FINDING MY FATHER

One Man's Search for Identity

BOOKS BY ROD McKUEN

PROSE
Finding My Father

POETRY
And Autumn Came
Stanyan Street & Other Sorrows
Listen to the Warm
Lonesome Cities
In Someone's Shadow
Caught in the Quiet
Fields of Wonder
And to Each Season
Come to Me in Silence
Moment to Moment
Celebrations of the Heart
Beyond the Boardwalk
The Sea Around Me . . . The Hills Above

COLLECTED POEMS
Twelve Years of Christmas
A Man Alone
With Love . . .
The Carols of Christmas
Seasons in the Sun
Alone
The Rod McKuen Omnibus

COLLECTED LYRICS
New Ballads
Pastorale
The Songs of Rod McKuen
Grand Tour

MUSIC COLLECTIONS
The Annotated Rod McKuen Songbook
Piano Sonatas

FINDING MY FATHER
One Man's Search for Identity

Rod McKuen

CHEVAL BOOKS • COWARD, McCANN & GEOGHEGAN, INC.

Second Impression

Copyright © 1976 by Rod McKuen

Copyright © 1967, 1968, 1970, 1971 by Editions Chanson Co.
Copyright © 1969, 1970, 1971, 1972, 1973,1974, 1976 by Montcalm Productions
Copyright © 1971, 1974, 1975 by Rod McKuen and Montcalm Productions
Copyright © 1966, 1967, 1968, 1975 by Rod McKuen
Copyright © 1964, 1966 by Stanyan Music
Copyright © 1967 by Warm Music

"When I Was Nine" was first published in the *Ladies' Home Journal*. It has since been rewritten.

Published by Coward, McCann & Geoghegan, Inc.,
200 Madison Avenue, New York, N.Y. 10016
and Cheval Books,
8440 Santa Monica Boulevard, Los Angeles, California 90069

SBN: 698-10774-8

Library of Congress Cataloging in Publication Data

McKuen, Rod.
  Finding my father.

  1. McKuen, Rod—Biography. I. Title.
PS3525.A264Z515   811'.5'4 [B]   76-20809.

PRINTED IN THE UNITED STATES OF AMERICA

The events in this book happened. Several of the locations and a few names have been changed to avoid embarrassing some of those people involved.

ACKNOWLEDGMENTS

The author gratefully acknowledges the help of the following people in preparing this text: William Martin Hooper, Bill Hooper, Jr., Gladys and Dewey Younger, Joy Orr, Laura Preece, Bill Preece, Jr., Jimmy Chamberlain, Pearl Pritchard, Ted and Frieda Woolever, Herb Caen, Wade Alexander, the Church of the Latter-day Saints Genealogy Library, Michael Hamel-Green, Hal Holman, Hilda and Jean Nielson, Claire Moseley, Jimmy Lyons and family, the Oakland, California, Police Department.

Photographic design by Hy Fujita.

All photographs not credited are from the author's personal collection.

AUTHOR'S NOTE

Since poetry has for so long been one of my main elements of expression I have at times included in this work certain excerpts from poetry triggered by an incident I was attempting to describe. This seemed to me more sensible than the tendency toward needless elaboration.

Some of the poems are new and were written expressly for this book; other poetry and song lyrics have been published before.

A list of sources and first lines for the selections appear at the end of the book.

Clarice Woolever

INTRODUCTION

During the 1975 calendar year according to one wire service more than half of the births recorded in America were illegitimate. The President of the United States is one of many people in or out of the limelight who was adopted and has no idea who his *natural* parents were. Yet in no country is there more prejudice, unkindness and abuse shown toward the unwanted or illegitimate child

The adoption laws in some states are so strict and unrealistic that infants and children will into their teens go begging for mothers and fathers. In some major cities there is such a shortage of adoptive children that so-called baby factories have been set up and flourish. Almost without exception when an adopted child decides at some point in his life to find out the true facts about himself, the adoptive parents feel threatened.

"Don't you love us?" is the question most often asked

by the adoptive parents of the adoptee who desires help in filling in that blank space way back in his or her early life. Naturally there are a few parents who don't feel threatened and are willing to help in such a search, but they remain the minority.

When children do go back and find out the truth about themselves, it can be much more unpleasant than the reality their new parents have made for them. Occasionally, an adoptee will find a whole new family and end up with two sets of good parents. Very occasionally.

But unless you were born or brought up under anything but ordinary circumstances it is impossible to understand how much some of us with no parents, one good parent, two bad parents, or even two exceptionally fine adoptive parents, need to know about their origins. To not know and be aware that something happened back there is to feel not only unwanted but incomplete.

If I'd known how difficult reliving my life for this book was going to be, I might not have written it. It wasn't that I didn't want to open any old wounds, the only wound I had had never healed. Certainly that was the reason I began looking for my father again after having given up the search so many years ago. No matter how medicinal the medicine of success, how comforting it's been to know that I was brought up, taken care of, and really loved by my mother, there was still that gap, that space that couldn't be filled until I knew something—anything, more about my father and myself.

I was born a bastard.

What connotation that word has—unwanted, unintended and, in a time when planned parenthood is all the rage, even unnecessary. But I have never looked in the mirror and thought of myself as a mistake nor have I for a long time now felt less a human being because of my dubious origins. Whatever my identity problems were, until her death four years ago, my mother was always able to solve them just by being there. She was a friend when I needed one, the truest counsel I ever had, a woman who would do anything to ensure I was brought up in the best way she knew how and never wanted for anything—especially love.

In my mid-teens when I discovered I'd been born out of wedlock, I began to seek information about my father. As I grew older, having looked in so many hundreds of directories and so many thousands of obituary columns, never finding a man who even *spelled* his name the same as me, I finally despaired of ever learning who he was. As my work—composing, writing, and performing—brought me more and more into the public eye, the questions I'd always asked my mother about my dad seemed increasingly painful to her till I began to think to myself, *Why not respect her wishes and give up looking.* That was the least I owed her for trying all these years to make me a decent human being. Even after her death and the terrible void it left in my life, I no longer pursued that phantom of a man who may or may not have been named McKuen, who might or might not be still living, who could or could not have known about me and, if so, did or didn't care.

Over the years, many stories and interviews have been printed about my origin, most of which I tried to keep from my mother. In that time, I've had perhaps two dozen "fathers" and/or relatives show up who, once carefully checked, turned out to be pranksters or worse.

About a year ago the need to fill in that blank section going back on my father's side began to intensify. I'd found two birth certificates—never having had *one* in my life—with some contradictory information. The first would have made me forty years old, the second forty-two. Since I had celebrated or lived through forty-one birthdays, I decided no matter what, I would believe the second. Besides, there are days when I feel all of forty-two and more; yet at the same time having never really had a proper childhood, there are those days and hours when I feel half that age.

In late 1975 when I began to actively look again, my friends almost immediately began to ask *why*. The why didn't merely address itself to my reasons for the search but went on to include—Why expose yourself by bringing up the past? Why risk by admitting to being a bastard whatever security or, as some called it, celebrity, you've attained?

What some of my friends didn't know was that all my life I've been looking in obituary columns, telephone books, around corners, hoping to find the man who more than forty years ago abandoned, was driven off, or didn't know about his expected child.

Every day of every year I've thought about my father, wondered if he were tall or short, intelligent or a man of common sense, beautiful to look at or plain, a criminal or a barrister, a teacher or a bum; or a retired gentleman jingling a gold watch in his pocket, the reward for threescore years of faithful service to the same company.

Suppose he needed me? Suppose he was in trouble and I could help? Selfishly I thought, *Wouldn't it be something after all these years to be able to help the man who helped to bring me into this world?* I need help too. I want to know who I am and what I am. It seems that everybody everywhere I go knows who I am but me.

I don't suppose unless you found yourself in the same circumstances or are very close to someone adopted or illegitimate, that I could tell you why I need to find my father; why no risk is too great and no amount of luxury or of material things or the satisfaction that comes from knowing there are certain things you can do and do pretty well, is enough to compensate for that gap back there somewhere that only one man in the world can fill.

This past November I met a man who was putting together a television documentary about people who were trying to find their relatives, many missing for as long as thirty years. Because of his ability as an investigative reporter, he was able to bring about the reunion of a number of families. Hearing about me from a mutual friend, he came to interview me, and before I quite knew what was happening, I had agreed to narrate the documentary and write the music for it. He, in turn, put me in touch with a firm of private detectives who would eventually help uncover a whole new world for me.

"Don't," said a friend. "Be careful," cautioned one of my few remaining relatives. "You're wasting a lot of time and money," offered my very conservative and careful accountant. I'm glad I didn't listen to anyone but myself in making the decision to go forward. The surprises and the outcome have been unbelievable. The newspaper accounts and publicity have caused parents, foster parents and adoptees to write me many hundreds of letters, most of them saying I'd helped them by not being afraid to come forward myself. Now the children would *ask* those parents or that parent. Now the parent would fill in the missing gaps.

Because of the bureaucratic walls I ran into in trying to open the files of so many years ago, one California assemblyman has asked my help in drafting a new bill that will make access, in this state at least, to personal records a lot easier for the adopted and those who need to know.

I don't believe that bastards are born. I know quite a few and it's taken most of them a great deal of effort and work to get there. I really believe that only liars and bunco artists are illegitimate. I try hard not to lie or put myself in a position where I have to question my motives. Still, like everyone else, I have my illegitimate days.

Why did I want to find my father? Know about him,

confront him face to face? I only wanted to say to him: "Look, Dad, everything turned out okay." Maybe he already knew that but I still wanted to find him. Look him in the eye and tell him myself.

R.M./1976

ONE . . . The Boy in Search of the Man

> The road turns here,
> up ahead you see it
> dissolving in the dust.

Rod, 1938

1

I was born in Oakland, California, at the Salvation Army home for unwed mothers, on April 29, 1933. The doctor, who is alive today at eighty-five, delivered me for $5. "In those days I must have delivered two or three a day at that price and he was just another baby." My father had left my mother before I was born and it seems to me as though I've always been looking for him. Since leaving that Salvation Army hospital everything else has been *up*.

My earliest memory is of being at the bottom of a high-walled crib and crying, both in the daylight and when it was dark.

I remember hearing children
in the street outside
above the noise
of pots and pans and bickering.

**They had their world
I had my room.
I envied them only
for the day-long sunshine
of their lives
and their fathers.
Mine I never knew.**

    I'm not sure when my mother told me my father had gone away, divorced her, or whether she said to me that he had died. I think it might have been after she married my stepfather and he began, for no apparent reason, to use me as a kind of punching bag. Maybe his brutality stemmed from envy because he had no son of his own. I think my mother told me of my real father so that I could dislike Bill without a guilty conscience.

    Until my mother married she supported me by working at a variety of odd jobs—waitress, barmaid, telephone operator, and clerk. I don't think I ever wanted for anything, and indeed the old pictures that survive seem always to show me in clean clothes even if my hair was bushy and my face dirty. Years later I was to find out that for a while I stayed with my Uncle Ted and Aunt Frieda while my mother worked, and that in the end the two women had fought over my returning to my mother shortly after she married my stepfather.

    Bill Hooper was a dark, good-looking man two-thirds Indian. If we were in the movies—and much of my childhood was spent in the movies—the part of my stepfather Bill would be played by Charles Bronson. Bill was not always mean, especially when he worked; his main occupation was as a cat-skinner leveling down roads on WPA projects throughout the western states. We went where the roads had to go . . . in one year living in seven different counties or towns, in Nevada: Ely, Winnemuca, Caliente, Pioche, Sparks. And finally, Alamo, where his mother and father had an old two-story house set on enough land to grow garden vegetables and enough acreage for me to get lost in.

While his father, George, was still alive I had some good times in Alamo. Every night I used to get paid by him for keeping quiet for five minutes. This became a tradition, so that when he'd see me coming at six o'clock he'd break out a buffalo nickel, hold it up for me to see, and whatever pretense for talking I'd chosen, I would stop immediately. Then I would eye the wall clock and watch it inch ever so slowly to the five-minute mark; once safe, I'd let out a yell and run off barefoot to the grocery store and load up on licorice or Guess-Whats.

In the summertime I would lie in the furrows of the to-mato patch with a saltshaker and gorge myself on tomatoes right off the vine or accidentally drop a melon I was taking into the kitchen and, of course, *have* to eat it, carefully saving the seeds to plant for my own melon patch. My only chores were feeding the chickens and bringing in the eggs. Once I had a pet rabbit. It disappeared one day before mealtime and afterward—told what we'd had for dinner—I resolved never to keep another domestic pet in Alamo.

Sometimes the irrigation ditch would overflow and drain into the field nearby, finding its way to the creek. Al-most every day I would go to the creek to look among the stones for crawdads or to trap minnows in the shallows. Re-membering my rabbit, I never let the crawdads or the min-nows find their way back home.

The old house seems bigger to me now in memory than it must have been. Outside it was weathered wood. The roof and nearby sheds including the outhouse were covered with green tarpaper. In the wintertime the roof leaked and some of the leaks could never be fixed, so that pings and plops into kitchen pots were an inevitable part of going to sleep on a rainy night. In the room I shared with my grandfather there were water stains on the wallpaper. After he had gone to sleep

I would cautiously peel off the first layer, then the second, till I came to the newspapers that had been pasted up first. I started teaching myself to read that way, and when my grandfather caught on, he began to help me each night. Soon, so much of the wallpaper was gone in so many places that I drew pictures on butcher paper and my grandfather whittled out wooden frames. And together we hung pictures over all the holes I'd made. It was our secret—nobody else ever knew. At night before we went to sleep, the two of us would remove the pictures one by one and go over the words and stories on the newspaper, and I would write down in a book words he explained to me that I knew I wouldn't remember the next day.

One day, sitting alone on the porch—everybody in Alamo had a screened porch—I was watching the rain far off in the distance, knowing that soon it would be raining in our yard and on the house. The thunder got nearer; suddenly, across the street a tall cottonwood tree that had stood there as long as anyone could remember was split right down the center by lightning.

A summer evening, thirty years or more ago, an ageless poplar pierced and sliced in half while I sat rocking on the porch swing, wet down by rain. Ever after that, or so it seemed, Grandpa would threaten us with lightning. If we didn't eat our creamed asparagus or boiled codfish, if we set out late for school, chased the chickens or stole tomatoes from the backyard garden, some blue-white flash

**would sneak up on us and cut
us down.**

**Lightning didn't doesn't
frighten me. Thunder did,
does.**

That September it was decided over my mother's ob-
jections that I should go to school. I was barely five but my
grandfather said I could pass for six or seven. So off I went.
That first school was three rooms, and I remember my mother crying as she walked away after turning me over to the
teacher.

Having had the benefit of my grandfather's help and
instructions, I was precocious and full of myself. Most of all I
was impatient at having to learn my abc's again and to finger-
paint; I had my own crayolas and with my grandfather's help I
had progressed far beyond fingerpainting. One day the teacher said something I didn't like and I called her an old cow. She
screamed at me, brought her ruler down hard across my
knuckles, and told me to get out. I did, but I didn't go home.
Instead I went to the creek, shared my peanut butter and jelly
sandwiches with the crawdads, spent the day trapping bees in
hollyhocks and chasing butterflies that wouldn't be caught.
Even after nightfall I didn't go home, knowing that the very
least awaiting me was my stepfather with a fresh-cut willow
switch.

As the sun was going down, I heard my name called repeatedly. Sometimes I knew it was my mother's voice, other
times I knew it was Bill's. But it seemed to me there were others calling too. Some I didn't recognize. I allowed myself to
fantasize that one was my father's. He was coming back to
take me and my mother away.

Finally, hungry and cold, I went home, sneaked into

the house, and tried to edge my way secretly to my room. I could hear Mama and Bill and his mother, Miranda, arguing in the kitchen. I could tell they were drinking. The argument was over me and I remember Bill saying, "He's your kid, I never wanted him in the first place." My grandfather came along, caught me listening, and motioned me toward the bedroom. I undressed and got in bed and he brought me dinner—codfish and asparagus, his favorites. God, I hated creamed codfish and liked asparagus only slightly better; but that night for the first time they tasted great.

The following day my mother woke me up and told me to dress for school. I told her more or less what had happened, naturally omitting the part about slandering the teacher. She'd already had a full report. I was surprised to find out that far from being mad at me, my mother was on my side, so off we went to the schoolhouse, where she confronted the teacher. They had heated words; the argument ended in my mother saying there'd be no need for me to go to school where I wasn't wanted because we'd be leaving Alamo that week anyway.

Suddenly, I would gladly have gone back to school, apologized, done anything the teacher said. The thought of moving had put me in a panic. I'd found a home, somebody who liked me and helped me and I was being taken away to God-knows-where, kidnapped in a sense by a stepfather who didn't care about me and a mother who loved him and had constantly to referee his feelings and mine.

When the time came to go I hid so I wouldn't have to say good-bye to my grandfather. We drove away from Alamo in his old Model T. In a way that was a comfort, because I was convinced we would have to come back to return it. We never did. And I never saw my step-grandfather again.

When I get back
to Alamo Junction
I bet they'll all
be pretty surprised
to find out just
how much that I've grown
and oh how worldly wise.

I'll tell them all
what kind of a world
waits beyond the trees.
I'll tell them all
the sights that I've seen
while hiking the highways
and sailing the seas.

Rod,
eight months,
Oakland, California.

Rod and Mom,
Oakland, 1934

I was born in a tenement
in nineteen thirty-three.
Mama sold her dances for a dime.
I never knew my daddy,
he never knew me.
Still they say I was singin'
all the time.

My mother, Clarice, had two sisters and two brothers, Ruth, Fern, Wesley, and Ted. All of them were born in Union, Oregon, with a difference of ten to twelve years between the oldest and youngest. When they were grown, Wesley married and stayed in Oregon with his family; Ruth and Fern moved to Oakland, and Ted, who was a seaman, sailed the world.

It was not really a close family, but my mother was the

youngest and she seemed to get along with everybody. Ted and Wesley, because they were brothers, were close, but Uncle Ted had very little use for Ruth or Fern. Even now, with him the only survivor, he refers to them as "meddlers" and "busybodies," says they were not trustworthy, and blames them for having run my father off the year I was born. At that time the three sisters lived together. Aunt Ruth was a fortune-teller, complete with crystal ball and handprinted cards: *"Madam Ruth—the Past—the Present—the Future."* Fern, the most inventive of the three, was for a time a bootlegger. Fern prospered, saved her money, and later was able to buy a business of her own.

I remember that Mama first worked in San Francisco for the telephone company as a long distance operator. When I was growing up she used to say from time to time that she could always get her license to be a PBX operator. She never did. After she left the telephone company, she became a taxi dancer and worked in the Rose Room and the Ali Baba in Oakland. I think it was there she met my father. Or she might have met him at the Stanford Hotel Cafe, where she had a job for a while as a waitress.

My uncle remembers coming home from a voyage and receiving a crisis call from Aunt Ruth insisting that he hurry to the East Bay. When he arrived, he not only found three sisters, but me, "the crisis" as well. During her last month of pregnancy, my mother had been taken by a friend to the Salvation Army home for wayward girls, where I was born. When she was well enough to leave the home, my mother politely thanked them for their help but insisted she didn't want them to make *any* attempt to find my father or check on my progress. From now on she would take care of me herself.

Mama moved away from her sisters and found an apartment. Ted and his wife, Frieda, begged to look after me while Mama was working and she reluctantly agreed. Six months or maybe a year later I left Uncle Ted and Aunt Frieda and went to live permanently with my mother.

Everyone who knew my mother and has any memory of that time has almost no recollection of my father. My two birth certificates say he was a refrigerator salesman, twenty-seven, named "Mack" McKuien or "Mac" McKuen. Mama was twenty-four and gave her occupation as waitress. Neither spelling of McKuien or McKuen appears in any of the telephone directories of that period in the San Francisco Bay Area. A first cousin remembers my dad as tall, good-looking and blond with wavy hair, she did not know his occupation— "No, all I know is he was a good dancer and rather quiet."

I never had a proper birth certificate until I was forced to get a passport for my first trip overseas as a civilian. My only identification until then was an Army record which I'd misplaced and a Social Security card. Both used the spelling McKuen. Without a birth certificate it was necessary for me to have a letter from my mother when I applied to the government for a passport. For some reason, she stated the date of my birth as 1935. I never bothered looking at the letter but was surprised to find that the first passport issued to me made me two years younger than I supposed I was.

Long before I had attempted to find a birth certificate in Oakland, California, under the name of McKuen; of course, there was none. It didn't occur to me until a couple of years ago that my mother, out of pride, might have registered me under her own maiden name, Woolever. When I did check with the Hall of Records in Oakland, I discovered the McKuien spelling of my father's name as well as a different version of his nickname. Thoroughly confusing. While I've never worried about age or felt entrapped by the youth cult, over the years I've had some interesting experiences concerning the year I was born. The first three or four editions of *Who's Who* I appear in have me born in 1938, and once a journalist in England listed all the various things that happened on my birthday in 1930.

Officially, I was born on April 29, 1933, and privately I've no desire to be older or younger.

My Uncle Wesley Woolever, who died a year and a half ago, said McKuen wasn't my father's name. I don't know how my uncle found that out. Another relative claims he was a married man and that my mother was protecting him. An acquaintance of my mother, who seems to have credentials enough to be credible, says he was of medium height, dark and almost Latin. Another: "He was well-to-do and had a family of his own." Other versions have him living in the East Bay area, "just passing through," and "from back East somewhere." *In the end, no two people remember the man in the same way.*

About ten years ago I began to believe that if he were ever real, he had since disappeared without a trace. Unfortunately, I never pursued to its logical end any reference my mother made to him during her lifetime.

**When I'd ask questions,
let's not talk about it now—
that's what Mama would say,
your Daddy was a long, long time ago
so I'd buy her presents
every Father's Day.**

I don't remember how old I was when my mother married Bill. He was almost always there. In one of the pictures Mama had, taken when I was very small, I was dressed in a sailor suit, a large arm reached out of one corner of the photograph holding onto my hand. I pretended that was Dad.

All through the 1930s it would have been hard to prove in any of the WPA camps around the country that the Depression was fast coming to an end. My mother, stepfa-

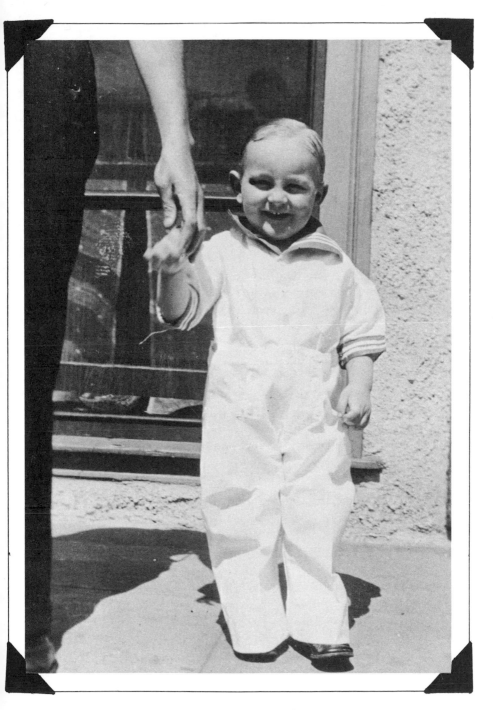

1936, Oakland, California
(I used to think the arm belonged to my father).

ther, and I were to know many such settlements in those days. After leaving Alamo and my grandfather's big house, our next lighting place was the WPA camp in Pioche, Nevada.

It was summer and I made friends easily with the people in the camp; most of my friends, even then, were older than me. Both Mama and Bill had jobs, Bill back in construction and Mama as a waitress and short-order cook. One day one of the boys was talking about his father and how much money he was making because he owned his own lumberyard.

"What does your dad do?" one of them said to me.

"Well, you see, I have *two* dads," I replied. "My stepfather has his own construction business." This, of course, was not true since Bill worked on a state construction gang.

"And my *real* father was a World War I flying ace. He was a colonel and after shooting down several dozen enemy planes was shot down himself. Of course, they sent us his medals."

That piece of fiction was the first big lie I remember telling about my father. Because he was intangible, and I knew little or nothing about him, I felt the need to invent a past for him to justify my own importance. Addicted to the movies—we used to see one nearly every night at the WPA camp—I secretly imagined my father as Tarzan, Clark Gable, or a Paul Bunyan-like character out of the North Woods.

Life in the camp was a little like being part of the circus. We lived in tents lit by kerosene lamps, and everybody knew everybody else. Some of the tents were permanent and had board floors—easy to scrub down and keep clean because of cracks in the boards. But most were pretty flimsy. Sometimes without warning, a wind would sweep through the camp, indiscriminately destroying every third or fourth dwelling. That only happened to a family once. Afterward fortifications were constructed that even a tornado would find hard to

breach. I remember being awakened sometimes in the middle
of the night when sparks from a coal-oil stove ignited one of
the houses in the tent city. Despite the valiant efforts of buck-
et brigades and would-be rescuers, once a tent caught fire
there was no putting it out. I don't remember anyone losing
their life but a family's meager possessions were likely to be
gone in moments.

For the kids tent life was an adventure. It seemed as
though we played endlessly. In the daytime, tag and sandlot
baseball, after dark, kick the can, run sheep run, and hide and
go seek.

Our family never seemed to have any money because
before my mother could intercept Bill's check, he would drink
or gamble it away. Still, I never remember going hungry.
Mama was a fantastic cook. Toward the end of the month she
would put dough in a frying pan and make it rise. She called it
a "whanniker," seasoned just right, it tasted every bit as good
to me as steak. Even now I like beans and stew, macaroni and
cheese and spaghetti much better than filet or any fancy cui-
sine.

Finally, when it was time for me to go back to school,
we moved again, revisiting yet another town I had known before, Caliente. Caliente was a whistle stop on the railroad. It
had a one-room schoolhouse and the first teacher I really remember—she was firm and strict and didn't take any nonsense. But she was full of jokes and fun to learn from. She
tried very hard to pull something out of our heads instead of
continually cramming things in. She was given to grand ges-
tures and unorthodox method. To illustrate a point one day
she went to the blackboard, picked up a piece of chalk and
scrawled the length of it: D–A–M–P–H–O–O–L.

"Any of you who don't understand what this is, it
means damn fool and any of you who want to take home tales
about my language can say I said, 'Goddamn fool!'" There was
an audible intake of air, and although I've forgotten what the

subject matter was, I will always remember the illustration.

Halfway through that school year we were to leave again for another town. But my mother had, at last satisfying Bill's wishes, become pregnant. The baby, a little girl, was born dead. Mama came out of the anesthesia just in time to see the child torn out of her. The attempted delivery had been so difficult that my mother was told never to try to have a child again.

I had been staying with friends of my mother's during the time she was in the hospital and it was agreed that, since they had school-age children of their own, I could finish out the term there. Bill and Clarice would move on to where the work was and later return for me. The job ended soon and they did come back.

The migration that had started ten years earlier with the Depression nobody knew was coming, was now in full swing. Was all America moving west? I don't remember ever meeting anyone else in my travels from California, Nevada or Oregon. Everybody we ran into seemed to have just arrived from Oklahoma, Minnesota, Nebraska, North and South Dakota, Florida, and the Everglades—and some from as far away as New York, Maine, and Connecticut.

To this day, people have a hard time placing my accent. In fact, I fall into accents easily. If I've been traveling in Texas a week I pick up a drawl; when visiting Canada I'm easily mistaken for a native and in later years after I lived in England, I came back home sounding like a "proper Englishman." I suppose that's because all my life I've met and mixed and mingled with people from everywhere. My roots were always wherever I had been the week before.

There was a certain camaraderie between all of the families in the thirties that were traveling around from job to job and circumstance to circumstance. I don't think most of us thought or believed we were living through the tail end of the Great Depression. Nobody really went hungry, especially

the kids. Booze was really plentiful, Prohibition had just ended, and while the kids played night games outside around the
tents, the adults were always laughing and drinking and making a ruckus inside.

Mama had found a job working nights as a barmaid,
and when Bill wasn't causing trouble at the bar, he'd sit at
home waiting for her return. Then, inflamed with what all of
us knew was unfounded jealousy, he'd start berating her as
soon as she came in the door. My mother was usually too
tired to fight for very long and undoubtedly had wearied over
the years of playing out the same scene with its painful dia-
logue again and again.

A little more than a year later we were living in Pioche,
Nevada, and my mother, still wanting to give my stepfather
his own child, ignored the doctor's previous warning and became pregnant again. Mama had an even more difficult time
with my brother Billy's birth. She nearly died, but Billy was
born at 8:30 P.M. on October 9, 1938, a healthy, normal boy.
At last my stepfather had his wish, a child of his own. Now I
can understand his point of view, but at the time I simply
thought to myself that at last I would have some relief from
his antagonism and beatings.

If there was any peace, it was to be relatively short-
lived, shattered by the arrival of Bill's mother, Grandmother
Hooper. To this day even Billy says she was the meanest
woman he ever met. Apparently, though, meanness agreed
with her, since she lived to be nearly a hundred. She received
a pension each month but we never saw it, almost from the
start it belonged to the slot machines. Mama would give her
money to buy food for Billy and myself while she was away at
work, and even that wound up being fed into any number of
the thousands of mechanical piggy banks in Nevada that seldom returned an investment.

When Bill was three months old he developed pneu-
monia and one of his lungs collapsed. I was left at home and

39

Bill, Clarice, Grandma Hooper, and Billy left in the sedan for the nearest hospital in Cedar City, Utah. While they were gone, Grandma's pension check came and I hid it behind the couch. Two weeks later when they came home my brother was much better. I was asked if any mail had come in their absence.

"No," I replied.

Obviously, Grandma Hooper didn't believe me and without much effort she found the envelope behind the couch. Immediately she began flailing away at me. My mother, trying to pull her from me, took most of the blows. That night I ran away from home for the first time—ostensibly to get away but, more importantly, resolved to find my real father. I kept a mental picture of this giant of a man returning with me on his shoulders and beating the hell out of my stepfather after he had kicked Grandma Hooper out of the house for good.

> **I do believe that for a while I have been an island to myself. Separated, adrift—though not set apart, dreaming still that tanned Tarzan will swing down from some tree and rescue me or that a dozen sirens will come singing as they form a bridge from this place to the mainland. The mainland would be to be not one, but *two*.**

Often I wonder
why we go on running.
There are
so few things pretty
left in life to see.

That is until tomorrow
when the crocus jumps up
back in California courtyards,
and you become
my back rest
and my English bible.

But I have run
And I have flown
Always away,

never *to* anything
and I am not sure
the running has as yet
or will ever
stop.

I don't believe
that I was born
            to run
or that I'm happier
while on the move
            or going,
only that the need
to be off and gone
occurs and reoccurs.

I'm not sure
that I'd stop still
            if I could,
or find a place
            and stay there.

There would always be
one more road ahead
one path not found
that should be.
Some place off beyond
some hidden bend,
better than
            the bend before.

Running away was to become a habit in those young
years. Of course, I was always returned, or as darkness fell,
came back by myself.

In 1939 we acquired another car—I think it was by dubious means, or it might have belonged to Uncle Tom. Everybody seemed to be headed north to Oregon and Washington where there was more work than in California and Nevada. Or if there wasn't more *work* there were more open jobs, because in California as many as three to five hundred families arrived every month. Shacks and lean-to towns were springing up everywhere. Along the Truckee in Northern California there were even people panning for gold. No one seemed to find any, though reports still circulated that gold was just below the surface or ready to come down the river when the next rain swelled its banks and started new tributaries.

Some settlers and migratory workers were smart enough to take advantage of government land grants and start small farming plots that soon became ten-, twenty-, and fifty-acre spreads. All the valleys around Los Angeles were becoming orange groves. In middle California, lettuce, carrots, potatoes, and beets were being harvested sometimes twice a year by migratory workers. (Most of the help came from Mexico and was paid very small wages, the real attraction being room and board.)

That year we moved north, too, stopping for a while in Union so Mama could visit Uncle Wesley. He and his family lived in a small house where I remember the kids slept three to a bed, head to foot. We weren't there long, but long enough for me to fall in love with the North Woods.

Further north we found a log cabin at the edge of a town that amounted to little more than a grocery store and a few houses but nevertheless qualified for a name—Scamania, Washington. The log cabin was so primitive it might have been built by Lincoln or out of giant Lincoln Logs. Not only was it deserted, but it had no floor and no door. Yet, when we moved in my mother quickly made it comfortable and home.

Again, I went back to school. Every day I started an hour early because the walk through the woods was long and I

43

Bill Hooper, Sr., Bill, Jr., Clarice,
Rod and Dog, 1939,
Bonneville Dam — Skamania, Washington.

Rod, Bill, Jr.,
and Clarice
1940.

Billy and Rod, ages about 2½ and 7½,
with Woolever cousins in Oregon.

needed a little extra time to spend with a new animal friend. A
mountain lion. He was curious enough to sit at some distance
from me and stare me down, twice a day on the way to school
and on the way back home as though prearranged. For the
better part of an autumn I used to find some kind of food or
present to bring him. At one point he ate out of my hand.
Another time I remember my brother petting him, much to
the horror of my mother, who stumbled upon the scene. Until then my lion had been a secret.

**It must have been
toward the first of spring
when I first saw him
a mountain lion sleek and soft
pretty as Rousseau might make him,
threading through the wood
padding slow
before he saw me
then stopping as I had
to look me up and down.**

**Perhaps it was the first time
I had been surveyed
by microscope or microscopic eye.**

**All that afternoon
we sat not twenty feet apart,
regarding one the other
till he loped off
in search of weasels
or a place of water.
I stayed there still
until the darkness
took the afternoon.
Then I went home,**

never speaking of the incident
till now.

I grew to know
the sorrow in his eyes
though never why;
but ever afterward I sought
that same, soft sadness
in the eyes of strangers
I would have for friends.

Perhaps that's why
my understanding friends are few
they lack a certain sadness
that betrays the truth.

We spent only one Christmas in Scamania. We must have had a little money because Bill told me I could have my choice—a sled or a blackboard for Christmas. I chose the blackboard because even then I wanted to write and draw pictures, and anyway most of the other kids had sleds I could borrow. My father called me a sissy, but when Christmas morning came, sure enough, I got my blackboard.

Christmas done, winter seemed to get harder. The log cabin just couldn't be kept warm enough and we knew we'd have to leave. Unless it was very cold and snowing, every morning before school and every afternoon when I returned home, I used to walk a mile or so along the highway collecting debris thrown from car windows—newspapers, matchbook covers, parts of magazines. I must have been beachcombing even then. Not having seen the ocean bordered by great stretches of sand, I gathered seashells and starfish made of tinfoil and brightly colored candy wrappers.

One day I met two men. They were amused at some-

one my age, in the middle of nowhere, walking along kicking
rocks ahead of him and stooping down for bits of trash. They
were hitchhiking and I fell in with them and walked awhile.
They questioned me about school and I told them I'd had
some. One asked me if there were any words I didn't understand and I replied, "Of course not." He said, "Have you ever
heard the word 'fuck'?" "No," I said, and I hadn't. I could
hardly wait to get back home and try out my expanded vocab-
ulary on my mother. She was aghast and promptly washed
out my mouth with lye soap. After that, before I tried out any
new words on my family, I auditioned them on others first.

And so we left
even as it rained
determined to be gone
before the snow could catch us.

The Model T had long ago
been traded off
to pay the grocery bill
so now we hitched to California

My mother with her thumb up
and her pretty smile
got us back down crooked roads
through Washington and Oregon,
along the California coast
and finally to Nevada.

I left behind the blackboard. The mountain lion reced-
ed in the forest, to come back often in my thoughts, as ride by
ride we inched through Washington, then Oregon and California and back to Nevada.

In North Las Vegas, we stayed with Bill's sister until

our welcome had been worn out. As soon as Mom started working we moved into our own small, rented house. These were leaner days. My brother and I would go to the store and ask the butcher for bones for our dog. We didn't have a dog. But beef bones, even with the meat scraped dry, were basis for gallons of good soup. And when Mama worked in a soda fountain near the North Las Vegas underpass, Billy and I used to steal pop bottles from the back of the store, come around to the front and sell them to the owner.

Now and then, the Lord provided.

Once in the middle of the night while coming home from an outing, Tom and Bill had been drinking. I think Tom was behind the wheel but the two brothers were arguing over who should be doing the driving. We were going pretty fast along a dark country road and suddenly we hit a cow. We stopped and got out to inspect the damage. The whole front end of the car was dented in. The cow was dead. I don't know how we did it but we got it into the back end of Tom's little, sawed-off pickup. That night Tom and my mother and Bill butchered it. Obviously none of us had an icebox big enough for the whole cow, so it was cut into pieces and placed in as many galvanized washtubs as we could find around the neighborhood and an attempt was made to preserve it with blocks of salt. For the next week our surrounding neighbors ate well.

In 1943 I ran away again. This time I got further than the town limits. I was ten and wanted to join the movies. Additionally, the hope that I would be better treated by Bill because he had a son of his own flesh and blood hadn't panned out.

I nearly made it to Los Angeles and Hollywood this time, but a boy that age hitchhiking soon runs out of stories to tell the motorists who pick him up, and eventually I was delivered to a police station in some unremembered town. My folks were notified and I was on my way back to Las Vegas. My schooling was still sporadic and I was a chronic truant, preferring to spend my time at the El Portal and Princess theaters attending matinees. At night, I'd act out scenes from the movies I'd seen that day for Billy. Mama was still working as a barmaid. It really used to upset her if Billy and I would come into the bar in the evening, and her most efficient method of getting rid of us was to give us money for yet more movies.

An even more ominous threat than my stepfather was Grandmother Hooper, who had now moved back in with us and had little compassion as far as I was concerned. On one of the rare days I did go to school I had to walk home through a field of tall grass and a gang of older boys who had been hiding there ambushed me and began to beat me up. At about that time Grandma Hooper passed by and, instead of coming to my defense, started egging them on.

It wasn't long before I'd run away from home again. My fantasy was still to join the movies. Taking money out of my mother's purse, I bought a ticket to Los Angeles. There were streetcars then that took you from the city to the valley. I spent the first day riding one out past Universal, Monogram, and Disney Studios. I tried to get into the Universal lot and was turned away, so I settled for another ride on the streetcar back downtown to Los Angeles. Nearly broke, I talked my way into a theater that was showing Bing Crosby in *Dixie*. Though I'd seen a lot of films, this was the first time I ever remember seeing Crosby. I knew that, along with Hawaiian music, he was my mother's favorite and I fantasized that my father had been Mr. Crosby. Well, he did have big ears. I sat through the movie twice looking for other resemblances.

At another all-night theater where the attraction was Olivia De Havilland in *Princess O'Rourke* I fell asleep and was shaken awake by a policeman, taken out of the movie house and to a juvenile detention home. An interrogation ensued, a

phone call to Nevada, and yet another Greyhound bus trip
back to Las Vegas.

I grew,
not necessarily erect.
I bent sometimes
but never to the lowest branch
and learned to love the smell
of people's bodies making love to me
as much as I loved lilacs.

I've always been attracted to older people. In the men I
knew I suppose I was looking for a father. One of the first sexual experiences I had was with a woman nearly three times
my age. Anyway, I always lived in an adult world. Even when
I went to school—however little schooling there was—it
seemed the children were taller than me. I was so impatient to
grow tall, I used to hang by my hands from the highest tree
branches I could reach in an attempt to stretch myself. Sometimes I hooked my feet underneath the bed and had my
brother pull my arms till they ached, convinced that I could
pull myself into being taller and older.

Las Vegas was the first place where I remember looking in a telephone book to see if I could find a man who
spelled his name M-c-K-u-e-n. By then, my mother had told
me my father's name. I was determined to call every McKuen
in the book to find out if I was related to them. Nobody in that
directory or any of the hundreds of others I thumbed through
during the next twenty years ever spelled his name that way.
But I never once thought there might have been an accident
in spelling or that my mother was misleading me, or that my
mother was anyone but my mother. And my father anyone
but a man who spelled his name M-c-K-u-e-n.

I read sometimes obituaries
in towns that I pass through
hoping I might find a man
who spells his name the same as me.
If he's dead then I'll know
where he lived and if he lived.

In the end
the songs I sing
are of my own making
          they mirror
what has happened to me
since I was abandoned
by my father and by love.

4

Mama canned currants
and mama canned peaches
and mama washed clothes by hand
and us kids had more
than the people next door
for we had a mama
who played the piano
and taught us to read
by the light of the lamp
a sailor man brought her
from some foreign land.

And I wish I were seven again,
I might even settle for ten
I wish I could go
to the Saturday show
and take the bus back home again.

Being a night person, most of the time Mom worked the swing shift in North Las Vegas, first in Lincoln Snyder's soda fountain and later as a barmaid in the Northside Tavern; but once in a while she would trade shifts, which meant that if it was summer and there was no school Billy and I would be free to go where we wanted to without much supervision. Our favorite place was the city dump.

If it was a weekend and there was no one around we could play on the tractors and cranes that moved the garbage and debris. During the week we'd slide on our bellies past mounds of garbage, hiding from the attendants, who would always chase us away.

One Christmas Eve one of the bartenders got drunk and couldn't report for work the next day so Mama worked a double shift. It was wonderful. We had the whole day and evening to play at the dump and it was our idea of a real Christmas. What treasures we found that day. A floor lamp, an easy chair with half the stuffing gone, an old box of somebody's discarded toys, old clothes, and more bottles than we could possibly carry to the market to redeem for the meager deposit.

Sometime during the afternoon it occurred to us as a surprise for Mom to redecorate the house with the furniture and odd bits of bric-a-brac we'd found at the dump. Billy had a red and yellow wagon and we must have made twenty trips, lugging all our goodies home. Of course, to make room for these treasures, we had to move all the furniture and trunks already in the house out into the front yard. While we were doing this, someone came by and thought we were having a rummage sale. I couldn't believe it when Billy came running in to tell me he'd been offered $5 for Mama's dresser. What a newfound source of money!

In just over two hours we were able to sell all the furniture we'd moved out onto the lawn, plus the curtains from the windows, pots and pans, and Mama's doilies. We even sold the oilcloth off the kitchen table for twenty-five cents.

It would be dark soon and so we had to complete our refurnishing before the light faded. I don't think either of us ever worked so hard. In the end we were both so tired we fell asleep on the nearly new torn satin bedspread we'd replaced on Mom's bed after selling off her comforter.

You can imagine her surprise when she came home from working two long shifts serving drinks to Christmas drunks and merrymakers. Perhaps "surprise" is not the correct word. I'm not sure what is.

Mama was too tired to spank us but she screamed and cried a lot. Though at the time we couldn't understand why. She had the new floor lamp—even if it didn't work, it could probably be fixed—and our latest kitchen table was larger than the old one. I had nearly mashed my thumb while hammering a two-by-four in to replace its missing leg. It now listed a bit, the angle wasn't so bad that utensils and plates would slide off. The curtains were much different from the old ones—while there were only three windows in the living room, there were now more than *twice* that many different kinds of curtains on them. And I distinctly remember Mama saying many times that she'd like to get rid of some of that old junk in the house just for a change—well, now she had her change. We hadn't yet found a replacement stove, but she had more than enough pots and pans.

Mom did look dazed, but she came to life again when she started to sit down on the new davenport. It collapsed completely under her, all three sides falling away. It was then that I handed her the envelope containing the money we'd received from the sale of the furniture: $71.30. It had been planned as a Christmas gift all along, and Billy had written in crayola on the outside of the envelope: *To: Mama, Merry Christmas—The Katzenjammer Kids.*

Mama didn't speak for a long time, but when she did she just looked up and said, "Merry Christmas." And it was.

Some of us were leaving
little towns and pretty places
(though we thought them ugly
                    at the time).

Not unlike the cabbage
grown for city market
there came a time to be detached
        and trucked away.
And we went willingly.

Some of us
went away
just to get away
some of us left
because horizons never stop.

Some of us were driven off
some of went driving off
and there were those
who couldn't do
or wouldn't do
what those who stayed behind
were left to do.

Some of us
chased shadows
      dreams
        ambitions
and as we went
we waved good-bye
      forever.

But whether we rode off
in coaches or in cattle cars
or crouched beneath cabooses
shitting railroad ties
that engines up ahead
had only just now eaten,
we were leaving.

Most of us without exception
had no predetermined destination,
there was some living
to be done,
even I knew that,
ever since they built the road.

Mama shrugged and let me go
with some misgiving,
and I suspect a little pride.

At eleven I finally left home and made it stick. I no longer wanted to "join the movies." I just wanted to get away. Away became Ely and Elko, Nevada. My first job was on a farm as a milk boy—room and board and a dollar six bits a week for carrying the milk pails to and from the barn and the kitchen in the main house. The couple I worked for had a spread big enough for a dozen or more hogs, ten cows, chickens, enough produce for themselves and the hired hands, and several acres of alfalfa. Later I learned to help bale the alfalfa after it was cut so it could be trucked to town and sold. Although I have always liked the autumn, I dreaded this yearly harvest—not because of the work, but because the machine that cut the alfalfa from its roots scythed everything else in its path. I would run ahead of the tractor, trying to frighten the field mice and rabbits out of the way. Despite my efforts, the mower always managed its share of mice, rabbits, several cats, and once even a dog. The dog lived and got around on three remaining legs. He became *my* dog and when I left that farm for a more lucrative job taking cattle out to pasture and staying with them all day, I took the dog with me. Each day we had to go a little further out, since the cattle mowed the grass so well. "The dog" as I called him, or "Here, dog, here dog," was the first I ever had. He came along with me to several different ranches I worked on and I finally left him in the care of the children of one of the foremen before I moved on to work on the rodeo circuit.

It was while tending cows that I began to write. First little more than words and thoughts that I couldn't make sense of or understand until I got them out of my head and on little scraps of paper. This led to my keeping a journal. Later, as a cowboy, in the bunkhouse at night, and when I worked in the lumber mills in Washington and Oregon my favorite radio program was *Your Hit Parade*. The next day I always tried to remember all the words to the songs Frank Sinatra, Lawrence Tibbett, or Joan Edwards sang. When I didn't remember a

Rod, thirteen, Ely, Nevada.

Rod, 1951 — Billings, Montana

Rod, 1950 — Oakland, California

stanza I'd improvise. Without knowing it I was starting to make up my own songs.

Elko winters were severe and there was always plenty to keep all of us busy. I was either breaking up ice in the irrigation ditches or working with a pick to widen them. Some days I'd get up before dawn to ride out and bring hay to stranded cattle. One year there was a particularly fierce Nevada blizzard and we were declared a disaster area. Hay had to be dropped from airplanes and thousands of livestock lost their lives.

That same year the "City of San Francisco" superliner that used to race down the railway tracks near enough to my window every night to make a shadow that would start at one end of the room, go all the way around it and out the other side, was derailed. All of us in the bunkhouse were jolted awake in the middle of the night by the crash. We got to the scene even before the rescue unit. Blood and bodies everywhere. It was my first real coming to terms with death and the inability to be of help or comfort to people in need.

The dead in an accident so sudden and without warning don't look dead. The hurt and dying seem bewildered. I was bewildered too. *My* train, the one I waited for each night, the one I hoped would one day take me somewhere, lay twisted, upended, dying.

If the winters in Elko were bad, summer could be just as extreme. Hot and muggy with only the cool evenings to provide some letup from the sun. Whenever there was an unusually dry spring, there was certain to be brush and forest fires. Most of us who worked on ranches in and around the area were part of the volunteer fire brigade. When the report of a fire reached us we would pack into pickup trucks and race off to the site. Fighting fires in those days was a lot more primitive than it is now. We didn't have the chemicals or helicopters that are almost indispensable to modern, scientific fire fighting. The best we could hope for was that the various fire breaks we'd plowed up earlier in the year would contain the fire within a few hundred acres. Often a good roaring blaze could leap twenty-five or fifty feet to the next patch of dry brush or timber.

**You can will the water to be still
the sea to stay as silent
as the unused tomb.
Command the heavens to be cloudless
and it can be so.
Ask the earth to honor quiet
and it will.**

**Only fire does not forget
nor does it let a man decide
its movement.
Fire is free.
That makes it able to enslave.
Fire is proud
or why else would it rave
on hillsides.**

In the summer while things were slow on the ranches, a few of us worked as spotters and forest rangers. It was during one such summer that I met Leonard. He was tall, though everybody seemed taller than me. He must have been six foot plus, husky, blond, probably older-looking than he was. He might have been ten years older than me or only five. We became close friends almost at once. Leonard had been everywhere. He had even bummed on freight trains and worked in rodeos. On night watch he'd tell me stories so vivid I could easily picture myself as Leonard actually living them out. I suppose, in looking back, I wanted more than anything to *be* Leonard. Not just his friend, but him.

It was Leonard who, when a rattlesnake bit me, took a

pocket knife, cut a wedge of flesh out of my leg, and sucked out the venom. I still have the scar. He was always the one who stood up for me when the older men on the ranch tried to push extra work off on me, razz me, or try to make me the butt of their humor. One particularly cold morning I got up and put my foot in my boot only to touch a fuzzy tarantula that had been hidden there. I was quick to pull my leg out but too petrified even to scream. Leonard found out who'd done it and beat the shit out of him.

Leonard's sense of humor was more to my liking. He was unbelievably agile and sometimes when I'd go looking for him I'd find him hiding in the most ridiculous places. I might be standing under a tree only to have him swing out of the branches over my head and fall at my feet pretending he was a dead cowboy or Indian—whichever role suited him that day. Other times we'd be walking along and for no accountable reason he would upend himself and walk on his hands for what could have been blocks, still carrying on a conversation and seemingly never tiring of handwalking. My only recourse was to attempt the same feat. *Attempt* is the operative word.

Leonard loved wildlife. Nobody knew the word "ecology" then, but he was very concerned about hunting and wouldn't have fired a gun at anything—anything alive, that is. He taught me how to skeet shoot, and often on Saturdays on our way into town we'd spend the morning at the rifle range knocking off clay pigeons.

Leonard had the kind of patience that would have made it possible for him to walk up and actually touch a wild animal. When he was satisfied the current ranchhands had no intention of harming them, he would always put food out, particularly in the wintertime, for deer, raccoons, coyotes, and even the gophers and ground squirrels.

The following spring, while attempting to cross the highway, Leonard was run down by a car and killed instantly. I remember going to see him in the Elko morgue. His head and feet were propped up on bottles. There was a towel over his belly and he looked incredibly white. I was amazed there were no scars on him. Still he didn't look real. Nor was it easy for me to believe that Leonard was dead, gone forever—not there to be my friend anymore.

I didn't touch him. I couldn't, but I stood for what seemed like hours just looking at him as he lay there. This man who had been so active was now so still that he resembled no one I had ever known before. He was not Leonard. Just a shell of somebody who looked like Leonard.

I guess Leonard and I had been playing games and that at my age I should have long ago given up kid games—I must have been nearly thirteen by then. But Leonard used to say to me that he was my brother, my uncle, and that, yes, he would be my father until I had found the one I was looking for. Then, if I didn't really like my father, he'd be my father all over again for real.

**I try to play as many games
as games there are.
To lie a little's not so bad
if it gets you through the night.**

Leonard got me through so many nights. We were friends, yes. He was my father, yes. We even experimented with sex together. He taught me how to ride. How to do somersaults. How to dive and swim better than I had before. He showed me how to ski the low hills in the wintertime, with only barrel staves for skis. And how to steer a sled around rocks and boulders on a ground covered with too-thin snow. When the ice thawed in the spring he showed me how to fish and how, if you were very careful, you could actually catch trout in little pools along the river with your bare hands. Before he died he had begun to teach me mathematics and spelling, both of which I hated till Leonard started exploring them with me. I'm not ashamed to admit I must have loved him. On the contrary, I'm pleased to be able to finally say it to myself.

> I do not lament
> the loss of innocence,
> the gain was payment
> far beyond imagining.

> And innocence
> is not too much to give
> to one who'd give you back
> the world.

> Down through my life
> I must be ever conscious
> of repayment,
> but to whom?

> Never mind
> I'll know the teller
> when he comes.
> Don't ask me how, I'll know,
> I'll know.

After Leonard's death I retreated more into myself. I got another job. It wasn't long before the authorities caught up with me. I'd been sending money home and I think Grandma Hooper got hold of one of my letters and turned it over to the juvenile authorities. I was brought before a judge and it was decided that at my age I shouldn't be running around the country on my own. The judge was even more convinced, though, that I shouldn't be living at home. After all, I'd been not only a runaway, but a consistent truant.

I was sent to the Nevada School of Industry—a reform school without walls—and in of all places, just outside Elko. So I was back in familiar territory. For a while I was the youngest boy there. The others ranged all the way to twenty with the exception of one twenty-six-year-old who was not too bright and stayed as a kind of unpaid hand, a bully to help keep some of the rest of us in line.

I never made any friends at NSI. Mostly I just kept out of the way—out of the way of the faculty, the superintendent, and the other boys who were intent on including me in their schemes that more often than not got me into trouble. Not only had I become more introverted with Leonard's death, but I was unwilling to think of anyone as a friend—certainly no one could be a substitute for the companionship and love Leonard had offered. I was growing up, perhaps faster than I wanted to, and I was growing up alone. But I didn't want it any other way.

I never felt in any way above the other inmates, but I did feel alienated and different and I was so alone that I was an easy target even in a crowd. At times it was as though I could stand outside myself and see me growing but not changing in any way and unable to alter what was happening. Everyone at the school obviously sensed my feelings, because after a while they stopped trying to make friends with me and every time a new boy was admitted he'd be warned that I was someone to stay away from. That suited me. More and more I began to take the fringe jobs even if they were among the dirtiest of the details—anything that I could do alone.

Adding to my discomfort was the fact that only a few miles away in an unmarked grave lay the closest friend I'd ever had. No one ever came to claim Leonard's body and he was buried in a pauper's cemetery, something I didn't know until I was returned to the school in Elko. Not even the other ranchhands had pitched in to buy him a proper funeral.

One of the officers or "instructors" in charge of the school was a tall, wiry, balding man about sixty. Brooding and sinister, he was the first man I was ever totally afraid of—including my stepfather, who, while he mistreated me, never terrified me. This man wouldn't listen. Being the youngest—though that changed soon enough—of perhaps twenty or thirty boys, I was an easy mark for blame whenever older members of the school had something to hide. I was almost always automatically punished either by a whipping, lockup, or restriction from going into town to the movies (our Saturday treat). No amount of pleading or protest on my part could change his mind. Yet I remember his saying again and again what a "fair" man he was.

It was frightening to come in from the field at the end of the day and see him in the fast disappearing light, silhouetted at the top of the steps leading to the dormitories. Always I wondered if he waited for me. He had the advantage. I had no way of knowing if I'd been accused of something that day that true or false would bring me punishment. Vividly I see him, even now, rocking back and forth on his toes, then his heels, still appearing rigid, chain smoking cigarettes down almost to his lips and staring off into nothing. Occasionally, when he talked to other members of the "faculty" he would laugh. His laugh was always short and direct, but it had a way of lighting up his face and made you wonder what it would be like if he really let go with a wide, sustaining grin.

The war was on during the nearly three years I spent at the Nevada School of Industry. When I left I had enough money in my pocket to get by on while I looked for some kind of work. One thing for sure, I had no intention of going home. All those years I had continued to see the lights flash by on the wall each night and I had hoped and prayed and wished myself on that train so often that I thought if ever I made it—if ever I were able to step down to the depot and board that train—I wouldn't even *ask* where it was going.

I came through
the clothesline maze of childhood
Up from the cities in the rain
if you wonder where it is I'm going
Well, I'm off on the hills
to catch the train.

Since Leonard had taught me to ride well and do a few tricks, after I was released from NSI, I wound up on the rodeo circuit. The cowboys in those days were incredible. Most of them were men and only a few of us could be considered boys. More often or not, when the chute was open and we came out of it, on Brahma or on horseback, loops above our heads, chasing a calf, we'd land on our heads in the dirt. The really good cowboys managed to stay in the saddle long after "time" was called. Somehow, though not among the best riders, I always made enough money for the entrance fee in the next rodeo in the next town. Once, while traveling through Billings, I ran into a man named Mac Ewen. Though his name was spelled differently than mine, physically and as far as his age was concerned, he could easily have been my father—except for one small detail—he had arrived from Scotland only a year before and his accent was as thick as the first Montana snowfall.

Being a rodeo bum is a free-wheeling life. At least it was then. A cowboy, whether astride the animal in the fairground or in the coliseum, or hitching down the road with a bedroll on his shoulder, commands a strange and deserved respect. Cowboys seem to be uncaring, moving through life at their own easy pace. Though some of them still compete in the arena long after they should be out to pasture, they never *seem* old. Maybe it's because all of us have been weaned on cowboy films and we secretly know they fulfill all the fantasies we ever had that none of us will come close to living out ourselves.

Brave
they straddle the animals,
hearts racing before the pistol sings
then leaping from the chute
man and animal as one
welded groin to back.

One small moment in the air
and then the mud.

Hats retrieved
Levi's dusted
back to the bull pen
to wait the next event.
Sunday's choirboys
in cowboy hats.

Huddled in the pits
below the grandstand
or lining at the telephone
to call home victories
they make a gentle picture.
Their billfolds bulging just enough
to make another entrance fee.

Next week Omaha or Dallas.
San Antonio is yet to come.
And now the Cheyenne autumn
like a golden thread
ties them till the weekend's done.

They wade through beer cans
piled ankle high in gutters—
the rodeo has moved
      down from the fairground
to the town
and every hotel door's ajar.

Better than the Mardi Gras.
The nights are longer than Alaska now
until the main event begins
    another afternoon.

The Main Event is still
to be a cowboy.
For ten minutes or ten years,
it's all the same.
You don't forget the Levi's
    hugging you all day
And Stetson hats
checked in passing windows
    cocked a certain way.

Some years later
when the bellies
flow over the belt loops
there's always mental photographs.
    Here the hero in midair.
Now the Dallas hotel room.
Now again the gaping tourists
licking off the Levi's
    with their eyes.
Photographs of feeling
    mirrored in the mind.

My specialty was bulldogging and I got so I did it pretty well. Leonard helped. He was always hanging somewhere in my head, coaching me and telling me what to do. And if he wasn't, then I wanted to be as good as I possibly could so that wherever he was, if he had any way of knowing, he could be sure I was trying hard for both of us. Leonard never got to be a *real* cowboy, and I suppose I didn't either. I was just pretending. Marking time. Filling up the days and nights until something *happened*. Anything. Those days, those years, I was always turning corners. Expecting. I was always rushing headlong down a block sure that at the end something waited. I was always traveling through time with a feeling that the good times were yet to come. Not once did I think that I was having good times then. But I was.

I'd like to be a lumberjack again
straddling high trees
        instead of high-born women.
Climbing heavenward among the branches
out of the well of meaningless words
I've fallen into from too much city living.

Trees are monuments to God
        cities monuments to man.
I need to meet my god again
among the ferns and trees.
There's too much *me* in my life
and not enough of *Him*.

And so I'd like to be a lumberjack again.

I left the rodeo after a freak accident that broke both my legs. The horse I was riding fell the wrong way, crushing my right leg and shattering the left. The chances of that happening in a riding or roping event are remote. I was young enough to recover quickly and once out of the hospital I was only on crutches a few weeks before I began to take my first steps and worked at getting back in shape again.

While I was laid up I started remembering how much I'd liked the North Woods. Memories of Scamania, Washington, and my own private mountain lion began to grow in my mind as memories of good times always do. I decided I'd head north to find out what kind of jobs there were in Oregon and Washington. When I arrived in Portland, I got myself a room at the YMCA where I stayed for about a week. Not much money was left after paying the hospital bills, so it was imperative I go to work soon. I scanned the want ads for jobs and went every day to the employment office, but nothing either the newspapers or the clerks came up with interested me. Finally, while standing in line to be interviewed for a job, I struck up a conversation with a Canuck who'd spent the better part of his life working in lumber camps. His description of the life was enough to immediately get me out on the highway, bedroll on my shoulder again, thumbing rides toward the tall trees that needed cutting.

There are enough different kinds of jobs in a logging camp and the crew is small and tight enough so that eventually, if you stay in one place for any period of time, you end up getting a chance to work at all of them. While I moved to several camps in the Northwest, I was still able to top, cut, load, haul, and loose logjams on the river. I tried my hand at everything—even worked as an apprentice cook, seeded acreage where the trees had been cut, cleared away scrub, and to get overtime tried my best at being a mechanic on the cars and trucks that needed servicing.

Logging can be a lonely life, especially if you are any distance from a town. Most of the time I was lucky and found a camp that was near something other than a roadside café or service station.

One camp was pretty much like another—a compound of five or six low wooden buildings. There was always a cook shack with a separate odor for each different time of day seeping through the mesh of a greasy screen door. A bigger building was used as a mess hall for meals and a recreation room at night. Usually there was enough work and extra money for double time so that the rec halls got very little use. The bunkhouses were long redwood structures with a coaloil stove at either end and rows of double bunks on either side between.

The camp I first worked in was more or less permanent and the drive to new timber was ten miles each way each day. It was an old CCC camp and the buildings had deteriorated since they were first thrown up. But inside, the dilapidated barracks seemed warmer than the bunkhouses I'd been in when I worked on ranches or even the dormitories of NSI. For one thing there was more space and various attempts had been made to make them homey—pictures on the wall, in my barrack a worn-out sofa and a rocking chair—and at least six wide windows looked out into the scrub just beyond the clearing.

> **Scrub pines struggle**
> **through the underbrush,**
> **sideways,**
>   **d**
>   **o**
>   **w**
>   **n,**
>   **up**
> **then   again,**
> **Never really heading skyward**

they seem happy to survive
if not to really thrive.

Nature never helps
the scrub pine tree
it seems to caution
get there on your own,
wherever *there* is.

I'm not sure
that even that slow-growing,
stunted, slanted scrub
could tell you
where it's heading
and which branch
        leads the way.

Scrub pines finally
find their way.
Proud, predictably
        unpredictable
they shoot up through
the underbrush
        and underbelly
of long grass
in their own good time.

        Try to help.
Clean and water down
        the root,
spread love
to the farthest limb.
It doesn't work
Their resilience lies

> in their own ability
> to go and grow alone.
>
> Straighten out
> a scrub pine tree
> and watch it
> snap back in your face
> even on a path
> you thought familiar
> and without peril.

I never thought in those days that I'd grow up so ecology-minded that I couldn't bear to cut down even the smallest sapling, though even then a giant tree thundering down in the middle of a forest was awesome and sad. Of all the jobs in a lumber camp that I liked, I think, belting up, shimmying up the trunk to top trees, then bumping, edging, thunking downward to the ground again was best. It was fun, too, to get out on the river and dance a logjam free—two, three men yelling warnings back and forth at each other, trying to be heard over the river's roar.

Though I probably wasn't aware of it, I had already become a loner. On paydays, if I rode with the others into town, I'd soon separate from them and go my own way, usually to a movie; later, the bars if they were dark enough so I wouldn't be recognized as a minor. Often I'd wind up back at camp after a long weekend just in time for Monday morning work. It's a wonder I survived those Mondays, having had little or no sleep on my weekend ramblings. Again, I was writing in what was now a journal, not so much a diary as a running commentary on how I felt at a given time. Many of the entries are undated, but nearly all start off with the hour and the minute.

Wednesday, 6:35 A.M. Trouble again—no rain in a month. Some fires reported in the North. They want to get all the

timber here cut by mid-month. I don't see how. Been rest-
less today. Don't know why. Dave was horsing around last
night and broke his foot. Serves the son-of-a-bitch right.
Guess he won't be bunkhopping in the middle of the night
for a while.

The above passage, while typical, hardly indicates any
move toward a literary style.

I don't remember who Dave was, but I have a good
idea what I was referring to by "bunkhopping" and "horsing
around." I can't remember a friend or name from that time
period. There are some first names in notebooks, but none of
them jog my memory to reveal that I had a friend who belonged or anyone I considered even an enemy. The lumber
camps, the roads leading to and from them, the logging towns,
come back graphically, but no names, no relationships.

I had a chance to hustle in the towns and I probably
did a few times. In fact, I know I did, but if it wasn't worth re-
membering in detail, it hardly seems worth mentioning.
Again, it was time to move on.

I was nearly sixteen when I came back to Oakland.
Having no place to go, I moved in with my Aunt Ruth, who
still read tea leaves occasionally for people down the block
and lived alternately on welfare and the money her twin sons
sent or brought home. By now I'd saved a few hundred dollars
and she helped me go through that before my mother, who
had left my stepfather in Las Vegas and was on her way to
Oakland, arrived.

After I'd spent my savings, my aunt had little use for
me and one day in a rage called me a bastard. My answer was
equally graphic and her reply was, "No, you really *are* a bastard." Raising her voice even louder, she told me that I had
been born out of wedlock, that nobody even knew who my father was, and I likely never *would* know.

I didn't say anything right away. I pretended not to hear. I couldn't even look at her. Finally I asked her to repeat what she'd said. On hearing the words a second time, I felt as though someone had kicked me in the stomach. On reflection I am never even sure why. Maybe because in reality, having nothing to go on in the way of tangible evidence of my father—no photographs, no ideas as to color of hair or eyes, height, weight, occupation—I had been able to invent and elaborate on the absolutely perfect father whenever I needed him. Over all the years he'd assumed various guises, various occupations. He was the captain of a ship or sailing vessel, the engineer or brakeman on a train. He was an actor who made movies, and most of the time he was a cowboy or a big, hardy man who worked out-of-doors. Now in a single sentence, a moment, he was no one. He didn't exist and as I walked out of my aunt's house for the last time the truth hammered me—I would probably never know him now, never see or find him and he would never find me. It didn't occur to me that my aunt might be lying. She had been so vicious in her statement, so positive, I must have known at once, intuitively, that she was telling the truth. And anyway, I received the news almost as if I'd been expecting some kind of revelation—a revelation that at last, however mean and inappropriate, had been given to me. I felt unhappy, betrayed, cheated, empty, lied-to, all at once.

My aunt's apartment was at basement level so that it was always dark inside and the only view of the street was of people's feet going back and forth in front of the windows. It was twilight when I walked out of that apartment for the last time, I was so confused and shaken I wasn't sure what I wanted or what I wanted to do. I only knew I had to get away from her and, if possible, from myself. That evening I walked for what seemed hours, aimlessly, with no destination. Finally I found myself at the edge of Lake Merritt. By now it was dark, a beautiful midsummer evening with a moon that scattered a path wide enough to be a highway across the surface of the lake. There seemed to be an infinite number of people out there walking that night. Some sitting on benches, some lounging on the grass, others seemed to just be standing looking into the water. I walked around the entire lake twice. By then I was so tired I sat down, laid my head back against the embankment, and went to sleep. I didn't wake up till morning. When I did, nothing had changed. It wasn't night anymore and there was no moon, but people went about their business, sitting or lounging or walking around the lake. It was still midsummer, I was still nearly sixteen, and still a bastard.

If I ever got over my aunt's telling me I was illegitimate or if I ever saw her again on friendly terms, I don't remember. I can't even remember the year she died.

When my mother arrived back in Oakland, separated from my stepfather, bringing with her Billy and just a couple of suitcases, she was a different woman. Heavier, she appeared tired, and the years of hard work she'd put in since I left her in Las Vegas showed. She was still beautiful, but seemed somehow beaten by life. Obviously she was desperately angry with my aunt for revealing what she herself had not yet said to me. She did say that she had planned to tell me the circumstances of my birth and I believe she had. I can never remember her telling me a lie. Not once. But my father was always a difficult subject for me to discuss with her. I don't know why. Maybe she was proud. He might have been married. He might have been someone she didn't like or liked too much ever to tell him she was pregnant. Though sixteen years before, there wasn't a popular women's liberation movement, my mother had still elected to bring me up on her own. Now she had come back to Oakland with my brother and the three of us were together. At least there was comfort and strength in that.

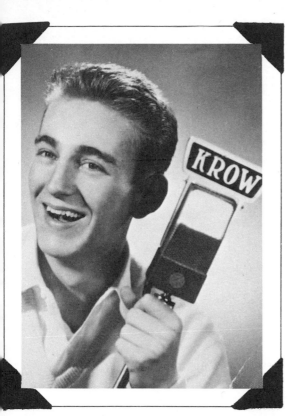

Rod —
Oakland, 1951.

As psychological
warfare scriptwriter
Tokyo, 1953

Korean Civil
Assistance Command
Taegu, Korea

7

On the 14th of July, 1961, my son Jean-Marc was born. His mother is French and lived most of her young life in the Camargue—the western part, or horse country, of France. His mother and I had very little in common other than the act that produced him. Certainly we were friends, but neither of us gave a thought to marriage.

So I, too, have a bastard son.

But Jean-Marc has never once been led to believe that he is less than human or different from other young people simply because his mother and father were convinced that a bad marriage between two people who weren't in love with each other would produce good parents. On reflection, I think not marrying his mother was one of the best decisions I ever made. Having over the years seen so many battered children, the victims of adults who took their hostility toward each other out on the innocents around them, I can't imagine two people joining their lives "for the sake of the children." One good parent is certainly worth more than two bad ones.

I see Jean-Marc often and, if I'm allowed a father's pride, he is one of the most intelligent, gifted, and nice people I know. His mother married shortly after the boy was born and his stepfather is a wonderful man and the kind of father every man should be. We're all of us good friends and my son once confided to me that he "had it so much better than all the other boys at school because he had two *real* fathers." (The italics for "real" are mine—but that's exactly how he spoke it and how I feel he meant it.)

I never considered abandoning Jean-Marc and his mother and I can't imagine why anyone would abandon a child they had fathered or given birth to. Perhaps that feeling of responsibility is the reason why I find it hard to believe my own father abandoned me. I still prefer to think he just didn't know about me. Jean-Marc is currently living and going to school in France and his mother and father—notice I don't use the word "step"—have promised me that when he completes his French education he can come to America to pursue his college studies.

I seldom refer, even to friends, to Jean-Marc's new last name or even his mother's first. A number of years back we had a very bad kidnap scare, and since kidnapping in some European countries is almost a major industry, I prefer for the time being to keep my son's whereabouts to myself.

Watching children grow
is like threatening the ivy
      to climb the garden wall.
You wait for it to happen
you hurry it along with love.
But still you're disappointed
at giving someone life enough

> to walk off on their own
> and not be carried in your arms.
>   You never turn your back—not once,
> and yet one day they've grown apart
>   or taller.
>
>   It's all the same.
> Polly put the kettle on we'll all have tea.
> Giving love to children
> has made us older overnight.

Growing older, I would eventually travel to nearly every state in the union and many countries abroad. And still look in telephone directories. I had no way of knowing that at forty plus I'd hire a private detective agency and they themselves would go through some two hundred Bay Area telephone directories, current and of the 1930 to 1933 period, and find only two spellings the same as my last name—a McKuen Moulding Company in Folsom and a woman who lived in Contra Costa Country—neither of whom, as it turned out, would be helpful in the search.

Having played so many one-nighters, lectured in universities, colleges, seminaries and given I don't know how many concerts around the world, I would be hard-pressed to say just how many directories, voting lists, lodge rosters, and obituaries I went through in the space of fifteen years or more. There were lists of McKuens but none spelled the way I spell it. There were:

MacEwan–MacKewn–MacKeown–MacKean
Macoon–McCune–McCuen–McCuan–
McCuin–McCuien–McKune–McKooen–
McCoon–McConn–McCowne–McKewen–

Rod McKuen

McKean–McEwen–McKewing–McKeean–
McKeown–McKeowen–McKeone–McKowne–
McKoon–McKeen–McKown–McKowen–
McKuhan–Macune–McQueen–McQuone–
McQuown.

Nowhere, but nowhere, would I find the spelling, McKuen, or even that one listed on one of my birth certificates as McKuien. Obviously my mother had made a mistake in the spelling, or perhaps, it was a mistake in the record-keeping back in those days. Once, when I first joined a performers' union, the American Guild of Variety Artists, I got my application form back saying I could not use the name Rod McKuen because it already belonged to a Chinese magician. A *Chinese* magician! I ignored their ruling.

In 1962 I returned home from living in New York for four years. With the exception of two brief visits to France, it was something of a forced return. I had lost my voice completely from singing rock-and-roll songs above a five-piece rock band night after night, month after month. During eighteen weeks of that period I did as many as four shows a night, seven nights a week. The inside of my throat was like raw meat. I was told I wouldn't sing, probably wouldn't even speak, again. Sure enough, I had to re-learn through long and exhaustive therapy how to form words so I could speak proper sentences, let alone sing.

Today, because I've toured so much and learned to sing from my diaphragm and not my throat, I've expanded a very small voice into a two-and-one-half octave range. Much of the credit for that would have to go to my conductors over the years, particularly Arthur Greenslade, Gene Palumbo, and Skip Redwine. Skip always insists that I sing the notes I've written and not slide past them or take the easy way out by going down an octave.

Just before I left California to live in New York, I met

Ed Habib and we became good friends. While I was away in the East he maintained a close relationship with my mother. Upon my return to California, he too helped coax me to sing again, and finally when I was ready, joined me as my road manager. Ed isn't one to stick with a job very long and he soon got tired of road managing and recording sessions. I was recording a lot now since my songs had taken a new direction and my writing was being discovered by other performers.

When I was ready to publish *Stanyan Street & Other Sorrows* Ed became general manager, shipping clerk, order writer, receptionist, etc., for the firm I started, to publish the book, Cheval/Stanyan Company. *Cheval* was named after the French word for horse—one of the first words my son ever spoke. And traveling in France, I used to collect sugar cubes from outdoor cafés, filling my pockets with them as souvenirs of where I'd been. When a waiter eyed me superciliously I would look at him blandly and respond, *pour mon cheval*. "Stanyan" was taken from the name of the street in San Francisco the long poem the book is based on.

My only means of advertising *Stanyan Street & Other Sorrows* was to record passages from it and to include on the album jackets the information that it was available by writing Box 2783, in Hollywood, California. It worked. To this day I've kept the box number. At first orders for the book trickled in for single copies. In less than a year stores were calling and writing for huge quantities. Ed nearly broke his back taking three or four carloads of books to the post office every day to be mailed all over the country. We had only two other employees in those days, Jesse Pearson (later to become the voice of *The Sea*, the first in a series of record albums I made with Anita Kerr) and Charlotte Ebi, who handled and still takes care of the copyrights to my songs and poetry.

Before Ed or I knew what had happened, we had sold 65,000 copies of the book from my basement and *Stanyan Street* was not only an underground bestseller but had made the established publishing houses sit up and take notice as well. I was offered a contract for a novel by Nan Talese of Random House, and having no novel ready I gave the title of a book of poetry I wanted to write. On the basis of the title, *Listen to the Warm*, I was given a $750 advance. To date, *Listen to the Warm* has sold more than two and a half million copies in hardback. When Nan asked if I would speak at a sales meeting prior to the book's publication, Ed came along with me to answer any questions they might have about the distribution end. Because the salesmen knew about *Stanyan Street*, I received such an enthusiastic reception that afterward I was asked if I would let them take over the publication of that book as well.

What did I want for it? I was asked. I replied there wasn't anything I needed. At that moment Ed kicked me under the table and said, "Yes there is. You want a Mercedes 250SL." I looked at him in disbelief. I had only learned to drive two years before, and the Mustang I'd leased seemed to get me where I wanted to go. Nevertheless, I turned over the publication of *Stanyan Street* for a blue 250SL Mercedes, which now has about 20,000 miles on it and which I still drive.

Ed and I went off to Europe for a series of concerts. By now he was acting in the dual capacity of manager and buffer, since I'd grown very cautious of crowds. I don't think anyone gets over being spotted in a crowd. When someone looks at me I still get the feeling my fly is open or my hair uncombed.

For some years I had been estranged from my own brother Billy, and Ed was becoming more and more a brother to me, someone I could lean on. I probably leaned on him too much because he soon decided that he preferred to go his own way. His concern for me never stopped, though, nor mine for him. It was just that he couldn't be buffer, manager, companion, and brother all at once. Our relationship has remained close and every once in a while he turns up.

Shortly before my mother's death she had taken steps

to adopt Ed—besides he was indeed now a part of the family.

Both of Ed's parents were long since gone, and despite the existence of some twelve brothers and sisters, Ed has always thought of us as his family. Mom wasn't even above disciplining him or scolding him as if he were her own child. I think Mom wanted me to have someone to take care of me. Little did she know that Ed with his various problems would be a bigger job for me to handle than my idiosyncrasies would be for him. Naturally that depends upon one's point of view. Ideally, brothers take care of each other, and both of us have become reconciled with my younger brother, Bill.

Before Mom could actually sign adoption papers making Ed my official brother, she died.

Certainly, though, I was still seeking my father. Neither of my brothers could serve as father surrogates nor did I want them to. But those long years of looking in the obituaries of every newspaper in every town I passed through and scanning those I-don't-know-how-many telephone directories only to come up emptyhanded had discouraged me and I eventually gave up hope of finding any kind of McKuen who would magically turn out to be the one. As my visibility increased over the years, I became busier and busier. Every time the telephone rang, a new fantasy for me to fulfill was projected by some promoter or agent, and my need to work seemed not to diminish but to intensify. It was almost as though I was trying to prove to myself that I could be just as good as anybody else by doing a number of different things. So what if I was illegitimate?

On a trip to Europe and my first visit to Scotland, after scoring the film *The Prime of Miss Jean Brodie*, I was greeted with such enthusiasm that complete strangers would walk up to me in the street and shake my hand. Some people even followed me into shops and offered to show me around, since I was a McKuen and obviously Scottish. (It didn't hurt that my song "Jean" had become almost a national folk song.

(One shopkeeper asked me if I had a Mckuen tartan and I said "No." I wasn't aware one existed.)

He replied, "If you are really a McKuen, however you spell your name, you're a Scotsman and you have a tartan." So I ordered a crest and a tartan. Some months later, back in California, I received a green-and-blue section of plaid with yellow-and-red stripes and a touch of black, mounted on a hardwood plaque. Raised upon that was a belt with a gold buckle surrounding an oak tree with two leaves emblazoned with the word *"reviriresco"* (I flourish again). Underneath, in hand-painted letters, is McKuen, spelled the way I spell it. Obviously they wanted to make their customer happy and they did. I have added this tartan plaque to what little McKuen memorabilia there is, including a MacEwen beer sign to prove that such a family did or does exist. Accompanying the plaque is a capsule history of the McKuen or MacEwen clan:

This clan were anciently known as the MacEwens of Otter, and a building known as MacEwens's Castle stood near Kilfinan on the shore of Loch Fyne. They were allied to the MacLachlans and the MacNeils, and in the 12th century owned part of Cowal. Ewen of Otter, from whom the clan takes its name, lived in the 13th century. About 1432 the Campbells acquired Otter and thereafter the power of the MacEwens declined. The name was later found in other parts of Scotland. The MacEwens were hereditary bonds to the Clan Campbell.

It would appear the McEwens were yet another clan gobbled up by the Campbells.

The following year I made my first trip to Ireland and once again people tried to be of help without even knowing I was looking for my father. The Irish were sure, however, that I was an Irishman, not a Scot.

"You don't even *look* like a Scot," one said.

To which I replied, "What does a Scot look like?"

"You don't want to know," he answered.

On my last trip to Dublin there was a bar/discotheque named Sloopy's after a poem of mine entitled "A Cat Named Sloopy." (Fame or notoriety takes odd forms. There is another bar in Salt Lake City called Stanyan Street, complete with blow-up pictures of me and a selection of my singles on their jukebox.)

Still, in Ireland as in Scotland, Australia, South Africa, New Zealand, Canada, Great Britain, Germany, France, Belgium, Holland, Utah and more than forty other states in America, there were no McKuens.

So even though my mother had died and could no longer be wounded by it, I did not resume my search. After all, I had so very little to go on. The two birth certificates with the two dates—1933 and 1935. The two spellings giving my father's nickname, "Mack" and "Mac." And the two spellings of his last name—on one document McKuien, and on the other, McKuen. My only surviving uncle had never met my father who, if he were alive now, would be in his late sixties or early seventies. There have been wars. Any number of terminal diseases might have claimed him. Worst of all, if the spelling of my last name was incorrect, there remained the possibility that no man named McKuen fathered me. Or even if he did, he might not have known about it. What hope was there in finding him?

I've said often that I never really knew what I wanted to do with my life. I started writing songs because I needed something personal to sing about. Writing poems was a way of expressing myself to myself. Performing was a way of tying everything together—not an ego trip but a way of reaching out. I always envied those kids who knew early on that they wanted to be doctors or dentists or scientists, songwriters, nurses, or whatever. I just assumed that if I wheeled straight ahead and worked very hard everything would take care of itself. I know that sounds simplistic, but for me it works.

Why with the opportunities I've had and the good fortune and what everybody else considers success would I still have a need to find my father? If you know who your own father is, I can't explain it to you. If your circumstances are like mine, I won't have to explain it. The need has always been there—not merely to fill in that blank space way back, but to find out why it is I'm here and what brings me to each step in my life.

Thinking back, I've had very little regimentation in my life—that is, after I left home. Certainly as an adult I've been lucky enough to work my professional life out on my own terms. Probably the closest I've come to any kind of forced discipline was during my Army hitch.

> **The bronze bellied men of war**
> **lie upon their narrow cots**
> **and search the ceiling**
> **oblivious to the**
> **wall of night.**

"You mens—you're in Uncle Sam's Army now and they's a few things Mr. Uncle Sam don't stand for." The top sergeant towered over us thick and mean, standing on a podium that made him seem like a not-so-jolly black giant.

"Racial and religious prejudices is so much shit and most of all there'll be no talking after lights are out. Last night somebody threw his gum in the urinal. You don't do that at home!"

In 1953 I volunteered for the draft to get my military service over with. I was sent to Fort Ord for sixteen weeks of basic training. Some of my friends who were already in the service bitched continuously about it, so I was determined I wouldn't. Jesus knows there was plenty to bitch about. On the hand grenade range a man blew his hand off. One morning the corporal who acted as postmaster was found hanged. In our eighth week, a drunken noncommissioned officer ran into a platoon on a night march and killed eight soldiers. Other assorted mayhem and maltreatment resulted in the company officers being called into a field house by the Inspector General to find out what in the hell was going on.

The ensuing investigation didn't bring anybody back to life, but it did bring about the transfer of all the officers connected with the outfit. Where they were transferred to, I don't know.

In boot camp I suffered from the usual lack of popularity that had dogged my life. During the first eight weeks we were not allowed to leave Fort Ord to go to nearby Monterey unless it was for emergency or religious reasons. Having gone through about three religions, I was at that stage of my life an Episcopalian. Episcopal services were conducted regularly every Sunday at Fort Ord along with Catholic, Protestant, and Jewish. However, it occurred to me that the closest Buddhist services were held in Monterey. For eight weekends I became a Buddhist. While I managed to pull the wool over the company commander's eyes, collecting my weekly pass into town, my fellow recruits were not amused. One Sunday evening after sneaking in late I was pounced on and had my head shaved. Not a very nice experience, but on reflection it did make me look more like a Buddhist.

At the end of my sixteen weeks' basic I was sent to Public Information School at Fort Slocum , New York, for an ad-

1954 — "First discovery" by Cobina Wright, Sr., at the Purple Onion, San Francisco.

1955 — Before leaving for the unemployment line, Los Angeles.

Photo Chuck Weedn

1956 — Hollywood. Things looking up! Columbia Pictures scholarship Universal contract.

1956 — San Francisco. After poetry reading at the Jazz Cellar with Allen Ginsberg.

In sequel to <u>Rock</u>, <u>Pretty Baby</u> Molly Bee gives me my first screen kiss in Universal's 1957 epic <u>Summer Love</u>.

ditional eight weeks' training. At the end of that time I found myself back on the West Coast and working on the camp newspaper at Fort Lawton outside of Seattle. Inevitably, orders came through for me to be transferred to Japan. For the next six months I worked as a public information specialist in Tokyo during the day and sang at Maxim's Night Club on the Ginza at night. This didn't go down well with the commanding officer and I was sent to Korea where I spent the remainder of my military service.

I was attached to the Korean Civic Assistance Command and worked out in the field showing films, pasting up posters, and giving out aid. Most of the little towns I visited had never seen a Caucasian before and the people were hospitable and welcomed me. Still, I missed singing.

In 1955 I received my discharge in San Francisco, and an old friend, Phyllis Diller, got me a job singing at the Purple Onion where she was working her first nightclub engagement. Phyllis was wonderful and down through the years has helped not only me but more people than she'd care to tell anyone about. Her heart is even bigger than her laugh.

The first of the many times I was "discovered" occurred when Cobina Wright, Sr., came into the club one night and suggested I come to Hollywood. The following week I was on a bus headed for Los Angeles.

Life as a protégé of Cobina's consisted of singing at parties. But I was singing and living comfortably off unemployment. One day I managed to hop a property truck that was on its way through the gates of Universal Studios. Once inside I crashed the office of talent director Jim Pratt. I think he was so taken aback at someone who would walk into his office and ask for a screen test that he had no choice but to give me one.

Over a period of two years I appeared in a series of forgettable films for Universal and was once asked to do a film entitled *The Haunted House on Hot Rod Hill.* I sent the script back to the front office with two words written on the cover. I was immediately put on suspension, which meant I couldn't work in any capacity in the entertainment industry. The film, incidentally, was retitled *Monster on the Campus,* and the part earmarked for me was given to Troy Donohue.

Shortly afterward I went to New York for a weekend and stayed four years. During that time I wrote songs, tried out for Broadway, wrote songs, made a few record albums, wrote songs, nearly starved to death, composed a different musical score for Albert McCleery's CBS Workshop every week, wrote songs, became a rock and roll singer and lost my voice, came back home to California, wrote songs, regained my voice slowly and most of all, I wrote songs.

While I was convalescing I decided that if I couldn't write and sing the kind of songs I wanted to, I really didn't want to be a performer at all. It was only then that the chain of events that would make the unbelievable happen and be believable, began.

Maybe I no longer thought about finding my father every day, but if I didn't it was only because some circumstance, real or manufactured, kept him from being in the forefront of my consciousness for every hour I lived.

Just now an earthquake moves beneath me.
Even as it ends, another shudder shakes
the ground. A California fact. An
anniversary almost of that quake two,
three years ago that jostled me from
bed at six and set the dogs to howling
and caused a crack to run eye-level
down the front room stairs.

I cannot be shaken up. If I could
I'd sway more willingly than most and
go whichever way the earth or some
mover of the earth thought I should go.

I've had my fist inside the world and
felt for sure I was its axis. I've seen
the kings go by, though I'll admit my
vantage point was from some distance.

For derring-do I've sailed through clouds
more easily than I once floated on a pond.
However jerry-built my life has been,
I've felt there was solidity of sorts.
In truth there is, however little.
I built what I thought needed building—
some would say security, I'd still say
solidity for some *one*.

There must have been a blueprint once.
Now, no trace of any master plan remains,
as nobody stops or stays here still.

I do not brood. I am not malcontent.
I am not. Where once I had opinions
good and bad of what I'd done. Even
to myself. I have no opinions now.

It, whatever that should be or is,
is over, never started or never was.
What I do have is this life, half built—
unfinished. Selfish though I can be,
it was never made for me. There are
takers, just that. But, as I go out,
there is no one here or up ahead
that I can give it to.

I wonder how long I can move, go through
the motions, knowing what I know. How

many years or days are left. Why go
through the motions anyway?

I don't know.

Do not think me sorry for myself.
I am not. I have, in fact, no
sense of self. But I am looking.

Universal's <u>Wild Heritage</u> 1958 — First starring role with Maureen O'Sullivan as mother (years later I would tell Sinatra I was his brother-in-law), and Will Rogers, Jr., who takes over after father is gunned down....

Here I'm pictured in macho pose with Judy Meredith. Though no photographs survive to document it, it should not go unnoticed that i gave Jill St. John her first screen kiss.

Universal suspension leads to "good life" in N.Y.C, three-flight walk up on 55th Street, 1961.

1962 — On board the Nieuw Amsterdam for Europe.

Paris 1965 — During initial collaboration period with Brel, Becaud, Aznavour and Frank Thomas.

TWO . . . The Man in Search of the Boy

Come now the bright red galleons
chopping through the seas
      of sensibility,
passing by and passing by.

Oarsmen at their oars
chained into believing
every voyage has its end,
every chain its weakest link.
But the sea's as endless
                  as the end
and galleons have been known
to meet themselves coming
        round again.

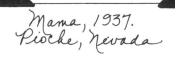

Mama early on.

Mama in her 30's probably taken in Nevada.

Mama, 1937. Pioche, Nevada

I'd rather be
a poet read
than one who postures
for posterity.
As I would rather *love*
and know that I am unloved
than be desired at a distance,
unmoved and unaware.
Having achieved as far I know
these two distinctions
the first has given me
happiness of some measure.
The second has made me
      not as sad
as some among you might believe.

I could not say exactly what day or even what year everything broke wide open for me. It seems as though one hour I had a small cult-like following of people who knew about my songs and my singing and vaguely that I wrote poetry. That I had lost my voice in the early sixties, regained it, started on a new career, made a dozen albums for nearly as many record labels, and written a few hundred songs. In the next hour seemingly everybody everywhere knew more about me than I knew about myself.

It's as if a button had been pushed and people were automatically turning my books and albums into million sellers. I was writing film scores and classical music, making hundreds of concert appearances a year, and traveling to every country I wanted to visit.

Some critics dismissed me as a flash in the pan, a poet on the scale of Kahlil Gibran or Robert Service. Others compared me to Yeats and Eliot and Browning. I was, in effect, in public domain, so much so that one year my jeans and sneakers put me on both the best and worst-dressed lists. I was winning awards and getting nominations—Grammy Awards for records, a Pulitzer nomination for classical music, Academy nominations for film scoring, Peabody and Emmy mentions for television—and I was the target for every would-be poet who turned to criticism for a living.

I think it must have been around 1968 that everything came together. That was the year three of my books, *Stanyan Street, Listen to the Warm,* and *Lonesome Cities,* were on *Publishers Weekly's* year-end top ten list. I had become the first author in seventy years of record-keeping ever to have three bestsellers in any one year.

At times I felt I no longer had a life of my own, and I remember one particularly tough period when I went through such an identity crisis that friends who came to my house were instructed by me to speak of Rod McKuen in the third person or leave him out of the room altogether. I'm not sure how I survived, but I did and do.

Aside from a musical special shortly after *Listen to the Warm* was published and guest spots on variety shows, I shunned American television and when I did appear it was usually on a talk show or to narrate documentaries or public service specials. Maybe I thought that television had such an inner eye that it would finally expose me as the introvert I really was.

In October of 1975 I was working in a nightclub in Denver called The Warehouse. One day I received a call from California reporting that a documentary filmmaker named Dick Carlson would like to interview me. He knew about my illegitimacy and thought my story might fit into a documentary film he was making about children in search of their origins. For the entire length of my engagement in Denver, I put off answering Carlson's call and, when I got back to California, I still made no effort to contact him, though his attempts to reach me continued. Certainly I was interested in his documentary, but perhaps the business of my illegitimacy had been dredged up enough. Why bother with it all again; what could it accomplish?

Finally, a next-door neighbor and friend, Milo Frank, who also turned out to be a friend of Carlson's, persuaded me to see him. The appointment was set. The hour arrived. Dick was at the door, punctual and full of enthusiasm. I liked him at once. More than that, we became quick friends.

Perhaps to set me at ease, or maybe because we trusted each other almost immediately, he told me about his own life and why he initiated the documentary. His father had died some time ago, and recently when he went back East to attend his mother's funeral, he came across a medical report while sorting out her papers and belongings that concerned a child remarkably like himself. After some delving, he learned for the first time that he had been adopted, a secret his adoptive parents had taken to their graves. Now married, with children, Dick still felt he wanted to know about his "real" parents. With the ingenuity and doggedness of an experienced investigative reporter he was able to track down his mother and determine that she was still living. More, he discovered that his mother and father had been neighbors. She was sixteen and the boy was barely seventeen. They were very much in love, but the pregnancy was obviously an embarrassment to the girl's family. She was sent away to have the baby. Neither the boy nor the girl dared tell the parents who the father was, and she was forced to give up her child for adoption. Less than two years later the boy shot himself.

For a while Dick decided not to see his newfound mother. Aside from coming to terms with it himself, it meant introducing a new grandparent to his children. They finally talked several times by telephone, but so far as I know a face-to-face meeting has yet to take place.

Despite the fact that his own personal tragedy inspired Dick to write and produce the documentary, he never included any of its details in the film. I don't think it was out of any apprehension, but more out of a need as the storyteller to detach himself from his subject matter and let the documentary work through the eyes and faces and feelings of those of us he finally filmed. He was probably right, and to my knowledge this is the first time anyone other than a few personal friends has ever heard about Dick Carlson's background.

After hearing Dick's story and the many others he had to tell of people he'd interviewed and seen and filmed for the documentary, I not only agreed to narrate it, but to write the musical score as well. In the course of our collaboration it was Dick who came up with the suggestion of hiring a private detective to find my father. And so in November, 1975, I made my first call to the San Francisco detective agency of Neilson & Green and a *new* search for my father began.

In December, 1975, Neilson & Green placed the following ad in several Bay Area newspapers:

"MAC" McKUEN
If you know of the above (spelling may vary) who worked in Bay Area in 1933 (then aged 27) as a salesman or CLARICE WOOLEVER (then 23) who worked as a dancer, waitress & phone oprtr. pls. call Neilson & Green. SF 665–4386.

It ran for several weeks and produced a number of leads, including responses from relatives I didn't know—first and second cousins, a great-aunt—all, of course, on mother's side of the family.

My mother was born Clarice Isabel Woolever, on September 28, 1909, in Union, Oregon. She was twenty-three in 1932. According to both birth certificates, my father's birth-

111

place was listed as the U.S.A. He was twenty seven (?) at the time of my birth, his occupation, refrigerator salesman, and the only other description of him is on Line 10 of the certificate: *Color or Race:* White. So much for in-depth birth certificates.

I first took the name Rod McKuen when I left home at eleven. I don't know anymore whether I invented its spelling or my mother gave it to me. Certainly my motive for having my own last name, whatever it was, was to have some kind of identity. I never felt any sense of belonging as Rodney Hooper. And once I knew my last name and was away from home, I felt free to use it. I would write it in notebooks just to see it on paper, and I remember how excited I was when I got my first payroll check made out to Rodney M. McKuen. Soon I had a Social Security card, and at eighteen when I registered for the draft, I shortened my first name to Rod so that legally ever since I've been Rod McKuen.

The first lead followed up seemed to indicate that my father was a salesman for Sherman Clay & Company in Oakland, now exclusively a chain of music stores. During the 1930s they sold all forms of appliances, including refrigerators.

A former employee remembered "Mack" McKuen as having worked there not only as a salesman but as a demonstrator of sheet music. When Hal Holman, the primary investigator assigned to my case, called and told me this, I was elated. *Suddenly my past connected.* My father had had musical abilities. The Sherman Clay lead came from the Booth Memorial Hospital file. However, that file also indicated that no contact had ever been made with my father by the hospital. So the following information must have come from my mother. He "seems to be well-educated." He was supposed to have lived at the Olympic Hotel in Oakland. He had not had any contact with my mother since September, 1932.

It took nearly an act of Congress to get any information out of Booth Memorial. It is still located at 2794 Garden

Street, Oakland, California. And its manager administrator, Mrs. Pearl Pritchard, while confirming that the hospital records did contain a file on Clarice Woolever pertaining to my birth, said there might be difficulties in making it available to the private detective. When she was told my mother had died in 1971 and they were representing the child who was eager to identify and locate his natural father, she said she needed a confirming phone call from me.

I did call Mrs. Pritchard.

I pleaded with her, tried to be as nice as possible, but she insisted on seeing a copy of my mother's death certificate and having a telegram from me. Once this was accomplished, Holman interviewed the administrator again on November 11. When he arrived she had a thick manila folder on her desk containing my mother's dossier. At no time was the investigator permitted to examine it directly. She would only read sections aloud to him. She indicated she was sympathetic to my position, but as administrator of a facility for the benefit of unwed mothers who desire their privacy, she had certain concerns.

The overriding factor in this instance was the expressed wish of my mother. Mrs. Pritchard was struck by the reluctance my mother had shown to having the father of the child involved in any way with his birth or upbringing. Since this was the precise wish of a former patient, Mrs. Pritchard felt she should abide by it. No matter that my mother had been dead four years, that my father had never been interviewed, never asked for protection, and that at my age I hardly needed shelter—that in fact I was asking that all the closets be opened on my early life.

After much pleading on Holman's part, Mrs. Pritchard agreed to talk about certain aspects of the file. She revealed all the supporting evidence that the birth certificate and hospital record provided. She added there had been no effort to prove the paternity, since Clarice Woolever had specifically requested no such attempt be made.

My mother had been brought to the hospital by a friend, but Mrs. Pritchard provided neither name nor address. When she was discharged she evidently had the choice of going to live with her sister Ruth or with the woman friend who'd accompanied her to the hospital. Mama had chosen the friend.

The file revealed an intelligent young woman. Clarice was also said to be "very nervous," so much so that the hospital staff had thought it best to honor her wishes not to get in touch with the father. Mom additionally insisted that all contact with the hospital be severed after she was discharged. So there was little or no follow-up on either mother or child.

The facts regarding McKuen's personal background were obviously sketchy, leading me to believe that Mom knew very little about him or had purposely chosen to keep whatever knowledge she had of him to herself.

What information there was confirmed the reluctance my mother had always shown to discuss my father. Here was the same woman, so many years before, evasive and adamant about not giving the social worker or clerk any more facts than she wanted to. Looking back, I see now that my mother was always a very private person. That was subconsciously the reason I never pressed her harder than I did.

The file included reports from social workers who had made various comments on her situation. Mrs. Pritchard was vague about these reports except to say that my mother had been described several times as a woman who had bleached hair. It also seemed that Mom had initially given the impression she was self-reliant, a little difficult to reason with, and bitter at her situation. But by the time she left the hospital she appeared to have softened. She was also said to be "devoted to her baby."

At this point Mrs. Pritchard decided she would go no further. Finally, she and the investigator made an agreement. If she could have an opportunity to meet me face-to-face, in order to better understand my true motive in wishing to find my father, she would supply additional information. Apparently it was not enough for her that I just had the need to know.

I'm not all that sure myself why it is I've always had the desire to meet the man who fathered me. I've never been bitter about him nor have I felt that he did me or my mother a disservice. How could I, with such slender evidence to go on? I think I really wanted to find him in order to satisfy something that might be lacking in each of us. Maybe he'd like to know what an incredible woman my mother was. I think I've wanted him to know that.

Explaining a feeling is like not having one.

> **Once I wrote a song**
> **almost.**
> **Sixteen lines that walked**
> **up from my belly to my head.**
>
> **As I stood waiting**
> **for the light to change**
> **and making up a melody,**
> **a yellow bus passed by—slowly.**
> **Looking up I lost the lines**
> **I thought I'd learned**
> **and several more that never came**
> **all because a bus passed by**
> **and someone smiled**
> **from out a yellow window.**
>
> **Buses pass by seldom now**
> **and horsemen not at all.**
> **Feelings fall around me**
> **but cannot be explained.**

I was able to convince Mrs. Pritchard by telephone that I had no intention of hurting my father, that my motives were honorable, and that I was perhaps old enough and just maybe intelligent enough to handle the situation should I confront him face-to-face. Mrs. Pritchard did make one condition: Should my father be located she would be advised before me, because if a formal contact were to be made, she felt it should initially come from her.

This request was no doubt based on her concern for the feelings of the natural father, should he not wish to be identified. The investigator had to go along with it. I, however, made no such deal. After all these years of waiting—and now suddenly finding a file in an obscure maternity home—I wasn't about to make any kind of bargain I couldn't live up to. Further, I was determined that if I had to I would go to the courts and get an injunction that would open the file for me.

While the investigator fidgeted and obviously showed his disappointment, Mrs. Pritchard added the scanty last details—Mother had been admitted to the hospital only one week before my birth, which according to her was unusual for those days. The friend who brought her there was Mrs. Margaret Stewart of 4434 Penniman Avenue, Oakland. There was some correspondence or an interview with Mrs. Stewart in which she described Clarice as a "strange girl—despondent and difficult to obtain information from." There was even a fear that Clarice might resort to taking her own life. The file indicated that her parents were unaware of her problem.

The wood holds dangers
darker than the dentist's chair
love is still the eye
of anything worthwhile
      or worth having
and so we keep that one eye open.

And knowing that it goes by
multitudes of attitudes and names

it's wise to learn and not forget
the favorite name for love is conscience.

But who can say
what conscience is.
Is it not letting on
        you care?
Is it not caring?
Is it holding back
        or letting go?

Conscience at the least
        is caring.
Certainly about yourself.

On June 12, 1933, about six weeks after I was born, my
mother left the hospital and went to live with Mrs. Stewart.
The only other information Mrs. Pritchard could provide was
that two other people had talked with my mother—one a hospital staff social worker, Mae Wilmer, now dead, the other a
Mrs. Elizabeth McCoy, who worked for the Alameda County
Charities Commission, a welfare organization. A letter from
Mrs. McCoy to the hospital in December, 1933, reported that
my mother had applied for financial assistance. In the letter
Mrs. McCoy asked for information about the father and said
that without it no financial help could be given. The last disclosure Mrs. Pritchard offered was that while she did not
know his first name, she was certain McKuien was the father
and "no one else could have been."

Now the investigator had a little more to go on. He began by looking up Mrs. Stewart. She had died four years ago
at ninety-six. The present owner of the house where she had
lived most of her life could add nothing. Later inquiries would
reveal that Margaret Stewart worked as a cook at the Alpine

117

Booth Memorial Home.

Rose Room photograph taken
New Year's Eve in 30's.

Hotel in Oakland in 1933 at the same time that Clarice Woolever reportedly worked there as a waitress.

Elizabeth McCoy was tracked down and described by a
friend as "a lovely little lady," who was already getting along
in years in those days. The woman who had known her was
certain that Mrs. McCoy had died many years before. There
were no records in the Alameda County Charities Commission's files to indicate that Clarice Woolever had ever asked
for assistance. However, many of the older files had long ago
been destroyed.

The ad was still running in the San Francisco *Chronicle and Examiner,* the Oakland *Tribune,* and a paper in
Reno, Nevada. More inquiries, leads, and calls were coming
in. Two mysterious letters were received, postmarked at the
San Francisco airport. Since only the telephone number of
the detective agency had been given, whoever sent the letters
had gone to the trouble of looking up the address in a directory. The letters consisted of the wrappings from a tobacco
product called Max Cigarettes and each had only four words
scrawled on the opposite side: CORRECT SPELLING IS
M-C-K-U-I-E-N. But they were immediately suspect, since the
first two ads that ran in the *Chronicle* had misspelled "Mack"
as "Max."

In early December Dick Carlson was finally ready to
film my narration for *Hello Again.* An NBC limo picked me
up one morning and took me to a home for unwed mothers in
Los Angeles. When I got there the camera and sound were all
set up and we began filming exterior shots. I had not seen the
script for the narration before, but I was pleased that Dick
had incorporated comments I'd made about my father, word-
for-word, into the script. What I wasn't prepared for was people walking about the set referring to my father as "Mack

McKuen." I mean, while I had known for some time that the man allegedly existed, no one had ever spoken his name in front of me.

It was a very emotional experience and a difficult day to get through. Late in the day we did more filming inside and the voice-overs for the rest of the documentary. I got home late, bushed. I wasn't in the house more than a few minutes when the telephone rang. It was a call from San Francisco.

"I think we've found your father," the voice on the other end of the line said.

"Where is he?" I asked. It was Holman.

"Well, we're either a day or a lifetime away from finding him."

It turned out, for the time being, that we were closer to the latter. They had tracked a man named Mack McKuien to Sherman Clay, despite the fact that old employee records had been destroyed long before. The current manager of the 14th and Clay branch of the store had put them in touch with the Sherman Clay president at the head office in Burlingame, a man named Donald Ravage. His secretary, Eileen Lyon, indicated a great willingness to assist in any way she could. Figuring the best chance of locating any information was to talk with some of the old-time employees, Eileen Lyon suggested several leads who in turn supplied more.

But where was the "revelation"? I already knew most of this information. Still, it did set me speculating again on my father as a piano player, his sleeves rolled up, a cigarette hanging out of his mouth, shaking his head sadly from side to side as he was forced to demonstrate songs he didn't like . . . nodding in approval and smiling to himself when he occasionally found a Berlin or Gershwin song that pleased him.

The more clues, real or unreal, I came upon the more personality traits and virtues I ascribed to my father. He was becoming for me more and more an urban man, who, while not too proud to sell refrigerators, nevertheless had his roots firmly in music. That, of course, explained my own musical tastes and ability.

But Eileen Lyon's leads came up mainly negative.

Vic Wykoff had not started working for Sherman Clay until 1936. He remembered no McKuien. Nor could Douglas Spencer, Jr., who was merchandising manager in the 1930s. Bill Lee, who had headed the refrigerator department at that time, had been dead many years. Kathryn and Sam Madge had both worked at the store in the late thirties. He was a repairman of musical instruments and she was in the payroll office. Neither could recall anyone by the name of McKuien or any similar names. Mrs. Madge did provide a black and white photograph but when the original was returned to her on December 18, together with photographs of me at the age my father would have been, they didn't remind her of anyone she might have seen forty years before.

Mrs. Edna Meyers, who played sheet music at the store, had no recollection of anyone named McKuien.

George Butler first went to work for Sherman Clay in 1930. He had many old photographs of store functions and employees but the earliest in his possession only went back as far as 1937. Again, like the other employees, he didn't recognize the name. He did know of a Mrs. Ringo, now eighty-eight, who had worked for the store and he believed she might have old copies of the Sherman Clay house organ, *The Harmony*.

On December 19, Butler had been in touch with Mary Ringo. However, the only issues of *The Harmony* in her possession were from 1920 to 1922. She did remember a man called Terrance McKeon. He had already been investigated. Since his name had popped up in San Francisco telephone directories and voter registries of the period, we had determined he was far too old to be the man on the birth certificate. Terrance McKeon died in about 1940.

Holman told me they had checked out half a dozen people who were refrigerator salesmen during the five-year period including 1933. None knew of my father or recognized his name. Inquiries were made of the Stanford Alumni Association to determine whether a Mack McKuien had ever attended the university. A search of their records determined not only that a McKuien had never gone to Stanford, but neither had anyone else whose last name started with McKu—.

The San Francisco Bay Area musicians' unions, Local 510 and Local 6, turned up nothing. According to back issues of the Oakland *Tribune* from July 16 to August 10 of 1932 (when it was determined I must have been conceived) several conventions were held in Oakland, some at the Alpine Hotel itself, and others whose delegates used the Alpine as a stopping place. They included the Annual Convention of the Pacific Society of Print House Small Craftsmen; the Annual Shriner's Convention (many thousands were expected to attend this one, and an aircraft carrier and several battleships were set to visit Oakland to be on display for the conventioneers); the Fourteenth Annual American Legion Convention; the Northern California Convention of the Seventh Day Adventists; and in Berkeley, the Sigma Phi Fraternity held its meeting on August 1.

I interrupted the detective, who'd been filling my head

with fascinating detail but had somehow strayed from his opening claim that my father had been found.

"I guess I meant, we're very, very close," he replied. "The leads are getting better. What I plan to do now is make a further check on the dance halls in San Francisco and Oakland. From what you've told me and from what I've gotten from witnesses who lived and worked in some of those places in the thirties, there seems little doubt your mother did work there."

More than anything, that phone call reminded me of the many times Mama talked nostalgically of her days as a dance hall hostess. For me the image was romantic, bringing to mind Larry Hart's lyrics for "Ten Cents a Dance."

In my late teens I went to my first burlesque show at the El Rey Theatre in East Oakland. The strippers all had exotic names, *Coffee Royal, Melba Toast,* and if you can believe it, *Norma Vincent Peal.* My favorite, and a perennial star, was *Tempest Storm,* "The Girl with the 44's"—and the legend didn't refer to guns. Her act consisted of a slow strip with pushups and squats and other calisthetics done while she alternately paced the floor in rhythm to "Night Train," sliding up and down the curtain on either side of the stage and letting out high-pitched squeals. She was *really* an exotic dancer!

While I was allegedly too young to be entering such establishments, usually if you had the price of admission few questions were asked. Like every boy of that age, I was curious about sex and anxious to get on with the promises of pleasure I'd always heard about, but that never seemed to be delivered.

Once I was talked into going to a dance hall, the idea being that there were perhaps "loose women" about and they were especially hot for *chicken.* I certainly qualified for chicken in every way, but I was amazed to learn that though the dance hall I visited was alive with girls and ladies of every possible age, none seemed very hot to trot with me or anyone else. They were not above milking your last couple of dollars for a roll of tickets or coaxing you into buying drinks for them (that looked suspiciously like tea), but beyond that they seemed so respectable as to be downright boring. I don't think the fact that my mother was a taxi dancer has influenced my memory in any way. On the contrary, the most memorable thing for me about those excursions was my excruciating embarassment. I have always been a poor dancer and can't even properly execute Arthur Murray's Magic Step.

The agency had turned up several leads on employees and customers of the dance halls. Photographs of my mother taken during the thirties were circulated to dance halls throughout the Bay Area and posters made and posted within several blocks of each one. On December 12, in response to the classified ad, a telephone call was received from Jimmy Lyons, former taxi driver and longtime East Bay resident. According to Lyons, he had known me for twenty-five years. True, in fact I had gone to school with his son, Al, and his daughter, Joanne.

More importantly, Jimmy and his wife were alive, had met my mother, and could easily identify her from photographs. Furthermore, when he was driving a cab in the 1930s, he knew many of the girls who worked as taxi dancers. But he could not remember my mother or the names of any of her alleged women friends from that time period. Lyons did recall two other girls who made their living dancing—one named Gilda and another Gloria. He suggested that the owner of an Oakland bar called The Ringside might know something about Gilda. Jimmy's memory was further jogged to include "Tuffy" Pierpoint, an ex-prizefighter and bartender in downtown Oakland during the thirties and Lola Carter, who used to be a taxi dancer. There was also Mel Simmons, an old-timer who still lives in Oakland and who might well have known people who visited the dance halls.

Jimmy even felt he had some fairly strong recollections of the name Mack McKuien. He thought he might have been a dance teacher, however; he couldn't be sure of the fact or even that the name of the man he was thinking of was actually spelled McKuien. When asked if he remembered anything about the old Olympic Hotel in Oakland, the last address given for Mack McKuien in hospital records, Lyons recalled that Max Baer, the ex-heavyweight champion of the world, used to stay at the Olympic in years gone by.

Gilda was tracked down, but she couldn't identify either a photograph of my mother or her name. She said that in the 1930s taxi dances were enormously popular and even on weeknights there might have been as many as two dozen or more girls working at the Rose Room alone. The turnover rate was high. Gilda wanted to be helpful and recalled that the three most popular halls in Oakland were the Rose Room, Danceland, and the Arcade.

I was sorry Gilda didn't remember my mother. It seemed to me that Mama *should* have had a friend named Gilda. The name evoked not only the dance halls but the gum-chewing, wisecracking best friend of the heroine in every backstage movie. In my mind the dance halls, the trolleys, the fashions, and the slang of the 1930s were as clear to me as if I'd invented them, instead of leaving it to Busby Berkeley.

George Grondona and his brother Walt used to own both the Rose Room and Danceland in the thirties. The surviving brother, George, is seventy. He had difficulty recalling those days. Gilda, Clarice, Arlene, and Mack failed to spark any response. Tuffy Pierpoint had been a member of the bartender's union in Oakland, but he hadn't been heard from in fifteen years. The owner of the Ringside Bar also remembered him but had lost track of his whereabouts.

Mel Simmons recognized both Tuffy and Gloria. He described Tuffy as a colorful character who would now be in his sixties and recalled that three or four years back he had gone to Hollywood to see about a possible film biography of his life. Gloria, taxi dancer, or "dime jigger" had been a friend of Simmons and he had last seen her working at the OK Toy and Novelty Store. But that had gone out of business a number of years ago, and he didn't know what had become of her. "Oakland has changed," he said.

I used to say that I only grew up to get out of Oakland. I'm not so sure that was true. The city doesn't bother me any more, if it ever did. I think that any bad feelings I had about it really had to do with what I was going through at the time, though. A lot of my problems while I was growing up were of my own making. Oakland is different and not just because of its juxtaposition to San Francisco.

Whatever I thought of it, Oakland was and remains a vital city. There in the thirties—being Clarice Woolever and "Mac" McKuien—must have been fun; the streetcars jammed, Model T's, Model A's, and Packards trumpeting at each other at every intersection, with Sundays reserved for a ride to Berkeley or Oakland if you had a car and a streetcar outing if you didn't. There were movies to see. Joan Crawford was enjoying great success in "a sound picture version of *Reunion in Vienna*." Charles Bickford and Richard Arlen, while not qualifying for that day's mantle of Redford and Newman, were paired in *Song of the Eagle*. Vic and Sade, Burns and Allen, and, of course, Jack Benny were on the radio—not to mention Amos 'n' Andy. Fannie Brice was Baby Snooks; Tommy Dorsey and Glenn Miller were yet to over-

Stanford Hotel.

Alpine Hotel.

Abbey Apartments!

Olympic Hotel.

1109 Madison Avenue.

take the popularity of Guy Lombardo and His Royal Canadians, or Al Bowlly. Bessie Smith had a cult following, mostly blacks; and 1933 produced some of the best popular songs ever written: Jerome Kern and Otto Harbach's "Yesterdays" and "Smoke Gets in Your Eyes"; Rodgers and Hart's "Lover"; Irving Berlin's "Easter Parade" and "Heat Wave." Johnny Burke wrote the lyrics to "Annie Doesn't Live Here Anymore," and Billy Hill penned three hits in a row: "In the Valley of the Moon," "The Old Spinning Wheel," and "The Last Roundup."

It was the year of "I Cover the Waterfront," "Temptation," "Shadow Waltz," "Love Is the Sweetest Thing," and "Did You Ever See a Dream Walking?"

Oakland was one of the great vaudeville towns, an even better place for artists to appear in than San Francisco. The year 1933 would see Will Mahoney, Tito Guizar, Jane Froman, Ruth St. Denis and Her Company of Dancers, and even Katharine Cornell at the Orpheum Theatre made it to beautiful downtown Oakland.

If I had been growing up in 1933 and not just being born, I probably would have had the same need to leave Oakland that I always did in later years. The great artery away from the city was the A train that went across the bridge to San Francisco. Sixteen years later it would become one of my greatest friends.

In 1933 Hitler's power was growing and he was seeking ties with Russia. But hotter news out here on the Coast was Joan Crawford citing mental cruelty, jealousy, and the fact that Douglas Fairbanks, Jr., "talked too much about nothing," in her successful divorce action. In the spring, the Swedish motor ship *Annie Johnson* had set sail for America with Greta Garbo. U.S. Custom officials assured the press that she would receive "no special treatment." Ronald Colman announced from Spain that he was thinking of retiring; and a national chain of department stores electrified Oakland with its dollar-day sale, which included new, cotton, daytime frocks, regularly $1.95, reduced to $1.44, two pairs of ruffled sash curtains for $1.00, a table lamp with shade, two playsuits, two long-line brassieres, four men's athletic shirts, a pair of broadcloth pajamas, six linen damask napkins, five training pants (with yoke front and French leg), or a dozen diapers—"$1, folks, only $1."

In the 1930s the Gildas and Glorias of Oakland's dance halls could buy silk stockings at three pairs for $1 and no one had heard of nylon. Palmolive was the beauty soap most stars preferred, and Pond's their favorite face cream. You could travel from San Francisco to Omaha for $64 or to Chicago for $80.50 and New York and points east on a round-trip ticket cost $135. The Bank of America had 410 branches, Britain backed France with its gold. A four-door Nash sedan with 116-inch wheelbase could be had for $695—factory fresh. A motor tune-up was expensive at $1.50. Bulova tried to market a "jump-hour" watch for men. Its main feature was no crystal to break; the hour, the minute, and the second were shown in three separate panels. The watches were unsuccessful and Bulova went back to more conventional timepieces. (The digital watch was not to reappear for nearly forty years.)

And the women of California were championed by Mrs. Walter Ferguson's revolutionary idea for women to celebrate Mother's Day: "Let's take the money that goes for gifts for our own most fortunate mothers and form a fund for that large group of American women, mothers too, who've suffered so tragically during the past few years from unemployment and poverty. They've kept homes together by the sheer power of faith and affection."

On April 21, while Amelia Earhart and Mrs. Franklin D. Roosevelt were flying over Washington and Baltimore, my mother was having labor pains and she was told I would probably be born that night.

Not till eight days later, on April 29, did I arrive. That

day there was an earthquake in Los Angeles, the United States mail service was being investigated, Teamsters Union officials were in the headlines because a gang had kidnapped two of them, financial columnists were ruminating over the instability of world currency, juvenile delinquency was a problem, and the headline in most morning papers was: STOCKS ROCKET 5 POINTS TO NEW HIGH OF THE YEAR IN THE WAKE OF INFLATION.

In the San Diego *Sun,* the first word in the crossword puzzle was "ode"—meaning a poem. Not given to courting coincidence, I haven't bothered to check the crossword puzzle in the Oakland *Tribune* for April 29, 1933. A variation on the old cliché might well be, *The only certainty in life is lack of change.*

**Straight lines are sometimes
difficult to walk
and good for little more
than proving that we're sober
on the highway.**

**I've never heard
the singing of the loon
but I'm told he sings
as pretty as the nightingale.**

**My dog likes oranges
but he'll eat apples too.**

Finally the long-anticipated preliminary report arrived
from the detective agency. It contained 173 pages of text, an

envelope of cassette recordings, an Oakland telephone directory for the year 1933, and two dozen exhibits ranging from
newspaper clippings to photographs, posters, and photo-
copies of death and birth certificates. At that time, they had
interviewed in person or by telephone thirty to fifty people,
and their leads had taken them all over California, to Canada,
Nevada, and as far east as Illinois and Pennsylvania. An interview I read with great interest was the one given on the telephone by my stepfather, Bill Hooper:

He is presently a self-employed plumber. He said he
and hs stepson, Rod, had never been particularly close to
each other, but he held no hard feelings toward him. As far
as he was concerned, Rod had always been a "pretty good
kid" who unfortunately fell in with the wrong crowd at a
young age.

Bill Sr. said he had been a Nevada man all his life.
His best recollection was that he first met Clarice Woolever
sometime around 1935 and they married in 1936. The first
time he encountered Clarice she was with a friend of hers
named "Loretta" at a dance hall or saloon in Austin, Nevada. Both girls worked there at the time and they also
shared a cabin. Loretta was tall, slim, had auburn hair, and
was attractive. She was about the same age as Clarice.

These two young women had told Bill Sr. that they
used to work together at a dance hall in the Bay Area. He
couldn't remember whether they mentioned Oakland or
San Francisco. One day they had been approached by
someone who offered them a similar job in Nevada at a
dance hall just about to open. The two girls had accepted
the offer, but on arriving in Nevada, they discovered that
the dance hall was actually a house of prostitution. Clarice
and her friend didn't want any part of that, said Bill Sr., so
they went to work for a saloon in Austin, Nevada, where
Clarice and Bill Sr. had eventually met.

Bill Sr. said he had not known Clarice for very long

before she told him she had a two-year-old boy. She made it no secret that her child had been born out of wedlock.

As Bill Sr. and Clarice became more serious about each other, young Rod's origins became more important to him. He was naturally curious about the child and the story Clarice had told him was essentially as follows:

She had "got mixed up with" this fellow McKuien while she and "Loretta" were working in the Bay Area. Clarice had "got drunk" and McKuien took her to a nearby hotel against her will and it was then that McKuien made her pregnant. Bill Sr. was not told the name of the hotel.

Bill Sr. was not certain whether Clarice ever had any further contact with McKuien. He did not know if McKuien even knew that he had made Clarice pregnant.

Bill Sr. agreed that Clarice may have embellished the events for reasons of her own, but his impression had been that she was honest and he had accepted her story as the truth.

He recalled that Clarice's two older sisters, Ruth and Fern, had taken a "protective" attitude toward her. He didn't know what had become of McKuien and had no additional information about his identity or whether or not McKuien was indeed the man's real name.

He then added that a man named King Todd had been a steady customer at the dance hall where Clarice had worked in Oakland and "was crazy about her," though she did not feel the same about him. Todd had come to see Clarice regularly at the dance hall. Bill Sr. also recalled that Todd used to write her letters. He could not recollect anything else about Todd.

He referred to a male friend of Clarice's sister, Fern. He could not think of his name, but recalled speaking with him on some occasion and he had received the definite impression that this man knew something about McKuien, perhaps that he had heard from Fern. Bill Sr. believed the man had been a steady boyfriend of Fern's for a long time and, at one point, had gone to South America.

Asked whether he had ever heard about a friend of Clarice's named Mrs. Stewart, Bill Sr. said he had and that she was probably close to sixty years old in the 1930s. He recalled that, after he married Clarice, they had visited Mrs. Stewart a few times in Albany, California, where she lived at the time. Bill Sr. was not sure how Clarice and Mrs. Stewart had become friends, but he remembered that Mrs. Stewart was always quite interested in young Rod.

Of course, reading my stepfather's transcript brought back memories. The really bad ones had somehow been tempered by time and age. And I remembered, for the first time in a long while, some of the things I admired about Bill Hooper. When he was sober he was often very good to my mother and I do believe he loved her. Often in a fit of remorse for some previous hostile action toward me, his way of compensation had been to give me an extra quarter for the movies or first crack at the bag of candy he got when he paid the grocery bill. Then too, he was very good to Billy. And my brother must have had the same sense of loss when he was taken from his father—even though he knew who he was and what he looked and acted like—as I had, not knowing my own.

I came very close to calling Bill after reading what he said. He had genuinely tried to be helpful and he too seemed to have mellowed. I no longer felt so much pain and rejection. I even thought that perhaps I understood how difficult it was for him in the beginning to be around a stepson of dubious origin.

Was I coming any closer to my goal? I didn't think so. Still, a lot of information was emerging—information I couldn't possibly have unearthed by myself. I sat quietly for a while with the report in front of me, my head full of mosaic pieces, trying to put some of them together. Nothing connected. There were only parts of a circle. Nothing connected at all. *I am here,* I thought. Someone had had to assist my mother in making me. If that someone was a criminal who'd

gotten a young girl drunk and attacked her, a bum just passing through, the man down the street leading a double life—
Mr. Hyde on Sunday morning, Dr. Jekyll Saturday night,
dead after a lifetime of guilt—or a gentle man seduced by a
woman who wanted a child but not a marriage, I still needed
to know. I went upstairs to the bedroom and it was a long time
before I went to sleep.

> We come into the world alone
> We go away the same.
> We're meant to spend
> the interlude between in closeness
>   Or so we tell ourselves.
> But it's a long way from
> the morning to the evening.

12

If columnist Herb Caen ever needs a demonstration of just how powerful his column is, he can point to the shock-waves that followed the one on December 18, 1975, in which he stated:

> FAMILY MAN: Perhaps you've been puzzling over the ad that's running in the classified section under Personals—"'MAC' McKUEN," it reads. "If you know of the above who worked in Bay Area in 1933 (then 27) as a sales-man, or Clarice Woolever (then 23), who worked as a danc-er, waitress & phone optr, pls. call Neilson & Green, SF 665-4386" . . . Neilson & Green are private detectives. Their client is America's No. 1 best-selling poet, Rod McKuen, who was born an illegitimate child at the Salva-tion Army Hosp. in Oakland in '33. His mother having died in '71, Rod is now hoping to get a line on his father, whom he has never seen.

The paper appeared in the morning. By that afternoon I had been contacted by *Time, Newsweek, People, Associated Press,* the New York *Times,* the San Francisco *Examiner* and in the following days, UPI, Reuters, and newspapers from London, Sydney, and Johannesburg called direct. All three television networks carried Caen's disclosure on their evening newscasts. Rona Barrett interviewed me for thirty minutes and seven of those minutes, expertly edited, were shown on the ABC morning television show. Two weeks in advance of their planned date, *People* printed an article they had prepared on me with its emphasis changed to my search for my father. KNX Radio in Los Angeles announced that they were preparing a Christmas Day special about my quest. It became the focal point for a *National Enquirer* article, and representatives of Dinah Shore, Merv Griffin, *The Tonight Show* and Sammy Davis Jr. all called offering me air time to assist in my search.

In addition to the still-to-come *Hello, Again,* NBC TV's Howard Miller devoted a full hour on the first Saturday night in January to a one-to-one interview about my need to find my father. The first magazine to reach me about writing a piece concerning the search was *Good Housekeeping.* Within days half a dozen monthlies approached me for first-person accounts of what was going on.

In many of the stories the office of Neilson & Green was mentioned and they received a considerable number of telephone calls and letters. In Australia it was front page news and kiosk posters shouted MILLIONAIRE POP STAR ILLEGITI-MATE, SEEKS FATHER. According to one London daily newspaper, I had had a complete mental and physical breakdown and more than 300 calls were coming in a day offering information or sympathy.

In point of fact, I had just had a physical examination and my health was perfect. My mental state couldn't have been better because I had decided to cancel about a hundred concerts for the coming year and this was the first real time I'd had at home in more than five years. I'd been here for nearly four months and wouldn't have to leave again till mid-March, then only over to London to record the score I'd completed for a film, followed by a few concerts in the U.S. in April, then I'd be home till late summer when I was scheduled to start another film. This time as an actor.

There had been a shuffling and reshuffling of personnel in my office—probably because I was at home more now. I was trying to straighten everything out at home and the office. Wherever I was, the telephone rang incessantly with new informants and information. Every mail brought new leads and offers of help.

In all fairness, the crank mail was at a minimum and I was buoyed by the fact that Green and Hal Holman both told me that nearly everyone they contacted seemed most anxious to help and those that knew of me and my work seemed to like it. Amid all the clippings that came in was an interview with a librarian in a prison outside Detroit who stated that my books and the dictionary were the most popular in the prison library and that prisoners quoted long passages from my work in their letters to people on the outside. A letter in *Publishers Weekly* responding to a previous article, written by a man apparently stating that a library needed only four poets, said that he would be at a loss to know whom to choose for the other two, since Shakespeare was a must because he was the most literate and Rod McKuen because he was the most popular. And the Orange County school system of California put out its fourth volume of poetry by students, *I Never Promised You a Rod McKuen.* A textbook appeared in the North Carolina school system entitled *I Don't Need You Anymore, Rod McKuen.* Again, it was made up of student poetry much of it modeled on my own.

For a month or more during all this, I averaged about

four hours' sleep a night, with no ill effects. Finally, I had to start declining work no matter how interesting or exciting each new proposition seemed to be.

Things at the office were in such turmoil that for a while I was without a manager, an office manager, and anyone to run the Cheval-Stanyan Companies I'd started more than ten years previously. Record and book contracts, domestic and foreign, were all coming up for renewal or change at the same time. Wade Alexander, the president of Stanyan Records, was pressed into acting as honcho in all departments; and Jay Allen, who handles the press for Stanyan and myself, was for the first time declining requests for interviews before even checking them out with me.

I was a little bemused by all the attention my renewed search was receiving, especially since I've never made it a secret that my father was a mystery to me, and I've said so often, "I was born a bastard—some people spend their entire lives becoming one," that it had become my personal cliché. Canadian broadcaster Larry Solwan said that if I never made another statement, that bit of philosophy would put me in the history books. (Though it works as a crutch, it hardly qualifies as philosophy.)

It is estimated that variations of AP, UPI, and Reuters stories appeared in nearly 3,000 newspapers around the world. Mail did flood in. At least one detective agency in Chicago guaranteed that they could find my father and were willing to do it on a contingency basis. Michael Hamel-Green's reply to this was, "Where were they when Patty Hearst was missing?"

A man claiming to be my father and presently living in Arkansas would have been thirteen when I was conceived, another from Milwaukee, nine. Various other dads turned up in Provo, Utah; St. Louis, Missouri; Rochester, New York; Jersey City, New Jersey; Birmingham, Alabama; North Dakota; Idaho; Ohio; Washington (both D.C. and state); and Auckland, New Zealand. While all this was happening I was made even crazier by the fact that I had two film scores to complete, a new book the publishers had asked me to promote, a half-finished book already contracted for, an opera I had been trying to complete for the past six months, an old screenplay I had written that had been resurrected by a new team of producers who wanted some rewrites from me, two record albums to make, and preparation to begin for my first assignment as a film director.

Add all of the above to a new strain of flu that was hand-carried to me from Australia and the fact that I was going to Sacramento twice a week with Milo Frank to lobby, rewrite, plead, and cajole a bill through the Senate that would protect the lives and ensure the safekeeping of animals featured in motion pictures.

I answered as much mail as I could, ran down nearly every lead I got, and the detective agency weeded out and worked on the more promising ones that had come from all this activity in the press and on the airwaves. For the past ten or twelve years I have retained Jay Allen as press agent not only for myself but for Stanyan Records and my other activities in general. Jay stood willing, and obviously able, to aid in getting coverage on my search, but we finally agreed that there had been coverage enough. If my father was alive he'd come forward. If he wasn't, I'd know soon enough. Besides, I wasn't seeking publicity—I was looking for my father. Though Jay did help, the decision to keep him out of it as much as possible was, I think, wise. Given an all-out campaign, the "Allen Machine" would probably have turned up a family in each and every state.

It was suggested, and with good reason, that I employ a firm or a host of somebodies to help answer the mail. Much of it remained unopened, unsorted. Boxes of it were brought to the house from the office almost daily and bags more were on their way. While there is no such thing as a typical letter,

143

there are some that had much in common and nearly all seemed difficult to answer in just a few words. A mother in Washington wrote:

> . . . I caught a snatch of conversation between you and Johnny Carson and I was very affected by it. My three children, very close to my heart and soul, are both adopted. I have a difficult time when I hear about people who feel their adopted family is not enough. They want "roots" or they want to know if they have brothers and sisters or hereditary diseases or emotional problems from their real parents. I really wish to hell I could understand. Please *help* me. I cringe when I see adoptive parents' feelings fade into the background. Aren't they human? What about their feelings? I fear the day when the ones I mentioned fully realize they are adopted. I want to understand the need some "special" people have (for "adopted" to me means special) to look for their biological parents. . . .

And from nearby Pasadena:

> Fourteen years ago I gave birth to a boy in a hospital section for unwed mothers, in Los Cruces. But when my ex-husband found out I was pregnant, he told me if I kept my son he would take my five-year-old daughter away from me. This he later did anyway. Now I have no son or daughter. I would like your help in finding out where my son is—not to get him back, but to let him know I love and I have never forgotten him for one day; and to tell him why I gave him away so that he will not have some of the emotional problems that some children have when they just think their mothers gave them away because they were not wanted.

From Massachusetts came the kind of letter I was to receive over and over again:

> With certain pain I read your "ad" as it appeared in *Newsweek*. You see, I too am a bastard, a term imposed

upon us by an embarrassed society. When I was twenty-one I discovered I was the product of a love affair between my mother (married) and another man. I also met my "father." That is all he is, "father" the great sperm thrower. You see, you'll find your nose and ears perhaps, but never your soul in the man who happened by chance to sire you.

And from England:

I hope you don't consider me impertinent in writing to you, but somehow I feel it could be my son in time to come, that is if I give birth to a boy in March this year. The father of my expected child and I have lived and loved together for two years. We desired a baby although the first few months of effort we were unsuccessful. Then the gift of love brought fruit and yet before it ripened he (the father) has left, gone. I know where he is, but what is the use of chasing dead love? None, let it die. Hopefully, I will tell my son the truth but I will be greatly hurt if he reveres his father too much. For what deserting father surely deserves the prodigal treatment in reverse?

Not understanding the language, it's difficult for me to know how the various accounts of my search were translated into Swedish—but something must surely have been lost in the translation; for while many of the letters I received were of a religious nature, no country brought forth such a burst of fire and brimstone as the letters and telegrams I received from Sweden:

REPENT! STOP. YOU FOOL. STOP. GOD IS YOUR ONLY FATHER. STOP.

How can you deny God? What has made you suddenly turn your back on Him? Don't you know that if you trust Him everything will turn out all right?

You are a bastard but you are the son of God. Your mother, if she is looking down from Heaven at you or look-

ing up from Hell, must be very hurt that you are going
against her wishes.

Say five Hail Mary's, three Acts of Contrition and
two Our Father's four times daily for a month and God will
take over your life and find your father for you.

A lady in Fargo, North Dakota, sent a wonderful typed
two-page letter. It was more than a fan letter, although she
confessed to having seen many of my concerts and to having
followed my career closely. The letter came on one of those
days when I was really down. It cheered me immensely.

. . . It hurts me when you refer to yourself as a bastard. I too am a bastard, if you will. It makes no difference to
me. That part of my life has nothing to do with me and what
I do with my life. However I feel that you were more fortunate than I because you were raised by your mother. I do
not know either parent, do not know what my ancestry is,
what nationality I am, and I was raised by two people who
adopted me and tried very hard to be good parents, but
didn't know how. I was born in a local hospital and was left
to be sent to the local orphanage for adoption. That was in
September 1914. I wasn't adopted until the following November 1915. As I wasn't very attractive to adoptive parents
they passed me by. Rod, please try to stop thinking of yourself as a bastard and think of yourself as Rod McKuen who
has inspired so many. I can't tell you adequately how you
have moved me, inspired me, and made it possible for me to
open up to life and really love. And that's my frustration,
love. I have so much life to live and so much to enjoy in
every way, even sexually (which I am now able to express
wholesomely) and so little time and no one who cares.

I felt like hopping the first plane to Fargo and hugging
the lady—wholesomely, of course.

From a small village in Britain, written in bold strokes and addressed simply to Rod McKuen, Poet, Singer, Writer, came the following:

> DEAR ROD,—Have you painted your heart and soul when asleep? I have! Many times. You have not seen your father? I have. But my mother is dead. I have seen my father, on other planets, in the caves of Ireland, in the countryside of England—in my dreams! I have a heart—I have a soul—I have a mind—But my health is dead. I have a wife—a family—but my future is dread. I have no wealth to ease my health. But my friend you are my vision of release, to let me live. To see many lands, each culture, each poetry, before I die. My heart says—"Please don't beg." But my mind says—"Please send me a beautiful cheque." Hope you see your dad, your real dad. Bless you.

There was really no hate mail but the closest thing to it might be a letter Rona Barrett received, addressed to me, after she interviewed me for *A.M. America*. It was one of the best interviews I had on my search, and according to ABC one of the longest uninterrupted interview segments Rona has done on the show. I reprint the letter to show what lengths people will go to just to bring a little nonsense into their lives when they could be doing so many other more useful things.

> DEAR RODDIE:
>   I caught your interview on the *A.M. America* program this morning and I wanted to tell you the truth about this whole business so you would finally shut up. I am your daddy and my name isn't McKuen either—it was just a name I gave that little chippy of a mother you have when I met her out here where men are men and not poets.
>   By the way, I told her if she had a little boy to call him Waddie and not Roddie because Waddie is a cowboy

name. I told her to spare the rod, but she was never any good at anything out of bed anyway.

You do have three half-sisters raised here in Galveston by a fine woman. Their names are Julie, Marie and Soapie. Julie is a professional stripper. Marie plays the mandolin and plays around if you know what I mean. And I can't get rid of Soapie no matter how hard I try.

If you want to meet them, I am sure they would be pleased to see you, but you would have to pay their way to California because they wouldn't want anybody in town to know they had a bastard poet for a half-brother, but I will send you their pictures for $10.00 each.

Love,
RENO
DAD

After Rona's interview many of the letters went to ABC directly in New York and some to David Hartman, the show's anchorman. David's an old friend and forwarded all the mail to me, including this excerpt I've taken from one of several letters written by the same person living in a small Alabama town:

DEAR MR. HARTMAN: I like your show. Please don't read this letter on TV. I was taking down our Christmas tree and wasn't really paying too much attention to anything when I heard the lady talking to a man. The man was trying to find his father. The lady asked if Mac McKuen would come forward. Well, that was what all my papa's friends called him. Mac. So you can figure out how I felt for a few minutes. I was stunned. Well, my father has been dead since August 1919. If you know how to contact this man who is looking for his father, will you give him this message: My father was a very good man who wouldn't want to hurt anyone. He had many friends who loved him. If it really was my father he was looking for I would like to meet him.

* * *

Well, having found two birth certificates, do you suppose there's a possibility that a third one exists? Assuming I was sired the very year of his death, it would only make me another thirteen years older.

Rod Steiger recently revealed on the *Merv Griffin Show* that he too was a bastard. Asked by Merv if he would attempt the same search as me, he replied, "Let me put it this way—if I was in a crowded restaurant and someone pointed out a man and said, 'That's your father,' the first thing I'd do is ask for separate checks."

Novenas were said in Australia, a mass for me and my father in Spain, various genealogy source books were suggested, the amount of money one has to send to the Bureau of Vital Statistics, at least seventeen mediums offered their services and twenty-one additional private detectives. I was directed to four cemeteries in four different parts of the country where people were sure I would find my father's tombstone. And many organizations who specialize in help of every kind offered me their services at no cost and assured me there were battalions of people at my beck and call. Because of my last name (whatever the spelling was thought to be), I was again and again referred to county seats in Ireland and Scotland.

To the mother in Washington: Don't be afraid that you'll lose the love of the children you adopted. The only danger you face is not being honest with your children. They *are* your children and will still love you even if they find a set of so-called original parents. I know you'll find that hard to believe but I promise you it's true.

To the woman in Pasadena: I hope Senator William Campbell will be successful with his bill now being considered in Sacramento that will enable people like you and me to trace relatives. At our age, whom are the bureaucrats protecting?

Rod McKuen

To "Massachusetts": Let me say the sperm-thrower did his share. I am not looking for my nose or ears or even my soul. I am looking for the man who "happened by chance" or otherwise to sire me.

To the lady in England who by now has a new "love child": Good for you, but don't deny the love you had for the child's father and, indeed, the gift of love that gave you your offspring. Certainly you are wise in not chasing a dead love, but any rancor or unhappiness you feel for your child's father shouldn't be passed along to the child. When it's time to tell the child, do it straightforwardly and let that child make up his or her own mind about the man who did his part in giving life.

To the good people of Sweden: I believe in God! And for my sake, not God's, will somebody please send me a literal translation of whatever appeared in your newspapers over there. Just for the record, I've never abandoned God, nor indeed would I presume on His time to help me in my search, and while I believe in prayer, perhaps only a little less than positive action, I try to use it as sparingly as possible. Having prayed on airplanes and made too many promises to remember let alone keep, I've decided that it isn't fair to waste God's time only when I feel threatened.

To the small village in Britain: Bless you too. Sorry about the cheque.

To Reno: Fuck off.

Most of all, to everybody concerned enough to write: It may take a long time, but at some point I'll get around to answering all your letters as best I can. That's a promise.

On December 20 a Mrs. Claire Moseley contacted Neilson & Green. She had read the Associated Press article in the Monterey *Herald*. She said she had noticed the headline several times before she got around to reading it. Then, when she saw the name Clarice Woolever, she "just about passed out" because Clarice had been a friend of hers forty years ago. When she knew my mother Mrs. Moseley's name was Fry. She is sixty-five years of age, in good health and working and still lives in the Bay Area.

On December 21 she was interviewed in her home. She remembers moving into a large apartment building in Oakland where Mama, Ruth, and Fern were already living. She thought the building was located on 9th Street near Oak. Also living with the sisters were Ruth's twin sons, Freddie and Richard, who were then about four or five. She says the five lived alone, no husbands or boyfriends with them. The build-

151

ing turns out to be the Abbey Apartments across from Madison Park in Oakland, and I myself think I remember going or living there.

Mrs. Moseley soon became quite friendly with the three women. My mother was close to her age and the two sisters were about ten years older. The friendship continued long after the women moved out of the Abbey into various other residences in Oakland. As she remembered it, Clarice and Fern later lived together in another apartment, while Ruth and the two boys lived elsewhere.

Mrs. Moseley recalls that it was while they were still living on 9th Street that Clarice took a job as a taxi dancer—at the Rose Room on 12th Street near Broadway. She added that Clarice had been "forced" into taking the job by her sisters. "I know that for a fact," she said. It was the Depression—times were tough and jobs scarce. She described Mama as a "beautiful girl" and said she was clearly the primary or sole source of income for all five for a considerable time. While she had difficulty in pinning down the exact time, she believes it was during this period that Mama became pregnant. "She never mentioned her pregnancy until she was 'showing' quite a bit; even then she was very closemouthed about the subject." Mrs. Moseley knew of a man named "Mac." Just like the one on my birth certificate. Again no last name.

She did know about the Alpine Hotel and wrote that that was where I'd been conceived. Over the years I've had to make friends with so many hotel rooms that it was actually a nice thought. She never said exactly who considered "Mac" my father—maybe she heard it from one of my aunts or from Mama herself. With all those women clucking away, it could have by then been common gossip. It wouldn't have been unusual for an unwed mother with a visible son to have the closest man in proximity to her whispered as the father.

Claire Moseley seemed credible as one of Mama's friends, and as I suspected, it did turn out to be Ruth and

Fern who told her "Mac" was my father. It was obvious Clarice's sisters were bitter about him. A pregnancy was a little inconvenient when it hobbled your meal ticket.

Mrs. Moseley wasn't sure, but she had the definite impression Ruth and Fern had been in touch with "Mac," had told him that he had the choice of being thrown in jail or leaving town. She also believed that "Mac" must have known he was the father of a child by Clarice. Her conviction was based mainly on the sisters' attitude. "After Fern and Ruth got through with him, he knew it."

This comment confirmed what my uncle had always told me: that my father had been driven away. Mrs. Moseley didn't know if Mama herself had ever been in touch with my dad after she became pregnant, nor did she know if they had met while Mama was a taxi dancer.

When asked whether she was confusing the Alpine with the Olympic Hotel referred to as the Mac McKuen residence in the Booth Memorial hospital records she insisted she was not. She pointed out that she had lived in East Oakland and knew exactly where the Alpine Hotel was. In addition, Mama had once told her that "this happened at the Alpine Hotel." No, she did not know if he had worked at Sherman Clay and she had never heard of Mrs. Margaret Stewart nor visited my mother when she was in the hospital. It had been her impression that Mama had lived with her sister Fern both before and after my birth. After my mother was released, Claire Moseley visited the two of us while we were living with Fern but she didn't recall any mention of my father. She thought I was perhaps a year and a half old when Mama left me behind and went to Nevada. She didn't see us again until I was perhaps four years old. By this time my mother had married Bill Hooper. She thinks it was probably about 1937 when Mom returned to Oakland, carrying another child by her new husband. This was the daughter my mother lost.

With no place to go and Bill out of a job, we had actually moved in with Claire, her husband, and their own little boy in Oakland. Times were still hard and jobs tight. After a couple of months of looking, Bill Hooper was unable to find work and we had moved on.

Another resident of the Abbey Apartments during the thirties, Mrs. Irma King, recalled, "We all lived in the same apartment house. This was during the bootleg days and the Depression. Everybody was broke and Clarice was the only one working in her family. She was feeding her two little nephews." Asked if Clarice had any regular men friends in those days, Mrs. King replied, "Clarice was not going with anybody—she was not going with a man, No, she lived right there where we did and she did not have a boyfriend. That's the reason we were shocked when it happened. It wouldn't have shocked us maybe if it had been somebody else, but Clarice was quiet and, as I said, worked every day and fed the rest of them. She was working at the Alpine Hotel when all this happened. Later on, Fern started bootlegging around the corner. You know, those were bootlegging days. You either bootlegged or you didn't eat."

Then Clarice "disappeared" for a while. Mrs. King asked her sisters what had happened to her and was given an evasive response about her "having gone out of town." It was not until one day when she went to visit the sisters and saw Ruth holding an infant on her lap that she said, "Oh my, when did this happen?" and learned for the first time that Clarice had been pregnant. Mrs. King said she had only heard my father referred to as McKuien, "That was the name she gave at the time Rodney was born. I don't think she knew the man. They were having a sales convention at the Alpine Hotel where Clarice was working and they went out. I was shocked when she showed up with Rodney and I helped take care of him. I don't even think the man knew he was the father of a child by Clarice. The spelling I always knew was M-c-K-u-e-n and they called him Mac. She probably met him at the restaurant there. But you wouldn't have known all that because they were keeping it shady until she showed up with the baby. The way I understand it, it was a conference, you know, a sales meeting was what they called it at that time. The girls at the hotel, the waitresses, went out to a party. Like I say, these were bootleg days. The only impression I got was that they went out and had too many drinks. I have believed that all these years. I have no reason to believe Clarice was forced to do anything against her will."

It doesn't matter much to me whether or not my mother was taken against her will or whether she gave herself to my father in an act of love. It does seem odd that so many people, including my uncle and even my stepfather, seemed to believe that Mama was indeed forced to make love to a man she had apparently no interest in. Obviously I would prefer to think that my mother and father knew and loved each other even for a night or a week. But I don't think the circumstances have any bearing on my mother's character and they have certainly caused me no pain or discomfort. The only real discomfort and feeling of isolation began and grew when I discovered I had no father at all—no man of substance to hang my hopes on, no one whose flesh and warmth I could turn to for security.

One thing seems certain though: my mother didn't want my father, whoever he was, to know about me. Mrs. King feels this might have been the reason why she went to such great lengths to hush the matter up. She says she once asked Clarice, "Why didn't you tell him?" Clarice replied, "Why should I make a fool of myself?" Mrs. King said that was the only conversation she ever had with my mother regarding my father.

Obviously I have consciously avoided speculating on whether or not my father ever knew or knows of my existence. I am not sure whether it's important. From all indications it was my mother's idea to leave, go away, or—even if he did know—not to stay with my father. If he wasn't aware of my mother's pregnancy, then quite probably she didn't want him to be. If it was rape, it went unreported. So I choose to hold the man who fathered me blameless just as I have never blamed my mother for not giving me more details about him.

If any blame should be assigned probably it should be assigned to me. After all, I didn't press my mother for facts when I could and probably should have, didn't attempt when I was younger and both my aunts were alive to ask them for information that might have been helpful to me and fore-stalled this lifelong search. It's hard for me to believe that Ruth and Fern drove Mac McKuen off. I suppose pride more than anything has made me choose to think my father was too strong a man to be intimidated by anyone.

If he *did* know about me, I think only my mother would have had the spirit and ability to convince him that she could take care of me by herself.

Though Mrs. Moseley maintains that my mother worked as a taxi dancer before I was born, Mrs. King is ada-mant that it didn't happen until after my birth. "She was not working as a taxi dancer when Rodney was born—that I can tell you. That was much later.

"Fern was a friend of mine and I'd moved to Alameda and married by that time, and so I took care of Rodney over in Alameda. Clarice was gone quite a while. They had to chase her down through the police department. We thought she had abandoned him at the time, but they did find her. Then she came back and got the boy. For a while Rodney stayed in Brisbane with his aunt and uncle, but apparently Ted's wife drove them out, so back they went to Oakland. The boy was just pushed around from pillar to post."

I find it hard to believe that my mother ever aban-doned me. After all she was resolved to have her baby and did so—pretty much on her own terms. Certainly she may have left me while she went to check out work but, other than her taxi dancing, I think Mama had stopped kicking up her heels and, in a strange way, had found certain roots in having a son who needed taking care of. In later years, whenever I needed her, my mother was always there. Although she never pushed herself into my life, she always applied the right amount of boosting and discipline in equal measure. I never went hungry and if my socks were darned and my jeans mended, they were always clean. I think she liked being a mother much more than being a wife.

Still I must have inherited my loner and wandering spirit from somewhere. If it wasn't from my father, then my mother's going from job to job would qualify as some basis for my own lifelong need to bolt when pressures become intolerable or a job I'm doing becomes boring. The closer I've come to Clarice and "Mac" on this journey, the more I think it must have been my legacy from *both* of them.

> **Sometimes I feel I've always been
> just passing through.
> On my way away, or toward.
> Shouting allelulias in an unseen choir
> or whispering fados down beneath my breath
> waiting for an echo not an answer.
> Everybody has the answers
> or they'll make them up for you.
> Just once I'd like to hear
> a brand new question.**

14

Sergeant White is an aide to the chief of police in Oakland, California. When the agency contacted him he expressed an immediate interest in the case. He said he knew my work and had several of my books, and he even indicated an appreciation of what he termed my "understandable interest" in my natural father.

White offered to do what he could to help, but candidly volunteered the obstacles: There was so little to go on: a questionable last name, no birth date, and only a remote chance they would find anything in their records without the help of a first name. In addition, it was the department's practice for reasons of space to purge the old records once an individual reached sixty-five.

Even if he should find some police record on the man, he might be restricted in releasing information. However, that was a hurdle to surmount when and if it actually existed.

Five days after being contacted, White sadly reported he had "struck out entirely" in his efforts to find something in the police records on either "Mac" McKuien or Clarice Woolever.

Additional investigation turned up a retired Oakland police officer named Jack Grasso. At sixty-six, Grasso was open and talkative and had a good memory of the thirties, but Clarice Woolever, "Mac" McKuien, King Todd, Arlene, Gloria, and so on failed to evoke any solid recollections. None of the photographs meant anything to him either, except for the one taken at a New Year's Eve party at the Rose Room in the early thirties. Grasso was able to pick out the Grondona brothers and Gilda, and he recognized half a dozen others, some of whom he was able to identify by name. In each case, however, he knew that the person had died. He was even sure he had gone to school with some of the men in the photograph. Many of the others looked familiar to him but he couldn't identify them positively after so long a time.

Grasso was twenty-one in 1930 and, being big and husky for his age, went to work as a "special officer" for the dance halls in Oakland (translate that as bouncer). In 1932 he began working for the Oakland Police Department where he continued until retiring after twenty-five years on the force. But during most of the thirties, he was a special officer in nearly every taxi-dance hall in the East Bay and came to know a great many people who lived in that nighttime microcosm— including the owners, dancers, and customers. He also boasted of knowing most of the pimps, winos, and whores of the period.

Grasso pointed out that it was not at all uncommon for the women who worked at the halls to hold down a second job as a waitress. The halls were frequented regularly by both single and married men. In the case of married men, it was common practice for them to use aliases, yet many were known to be married and didn't seem to care.

Whatever the dime-a-dance girl's reputation (and according to Grasso, a few were involved in more than taxi dancing), I doubt very much that my mother considered her job as a taxi dancer anything more than just that, a job. A way to support all of us. She did like dancing and never lost her enthusiasm for it. The snapshots I have of her as a flapper reveal a really pretty woman. I know from my uncle and others that she was very popular. But Mom was also reserved, in some ways *too* prim and proper. As difficult a time as my stepfather gave her, I am positive she never cheated on him. Infidelity to a man with whom she had exchanged marriage vows would have been alien to her.

As the dance halls in and around Oakland died out, they turned a little sleazy, a little tawdry, but I don't recall any of them being referred to as houses of prostitution. Even if Hollywood and movie memoirs like June Havoc's hadn't given us a picture of the halls of the period, they are not difficult to imagine. Close cousins to the crowded, noisy discotheques of today—but live music, not live DJ's playing canned music. People dancing with their arms around each other, not five feet apart, even music softer than the earplug level of today.

Hanging from the ceiling of the center of the hall would be the indispensable mirrored globe that, picked up by a spotlight, sent a thousand flecks and slivers of light around the room. The walls had tapestries and plush velvet curtains—the dimmer the light, the plusher the curtain. Bands worked in shifts, forty minutes at a time—and the favorite songs of the day interspersed with the dance hall standards were played a dozen times a night. The flappers weren't bigbusted bunnies. They were flat-chested by Hefner's standards and the style was "late slink." The dresses were usually onepiece affairs, lightweight, lots of fringe and beads, usually held on the girl's shoulders by slender straps. Some were downright shocking for the day, exposing half a bare back. Cleavage was not essential. But good legs were a definite asset, and a girl's pumps nearly always matched her dress.

The tiny bags, one-eighth the size of those women carry today, still had ample room for cosmetics for rouged lips, cheeks and even knees, plus enough change to redeem a lady many times a night for her trips to the powder room to renew and repair her face and move a glued sequin from the left to the right cheek or more often maneuver an artificial beauty mark until it was in exactly the right spot.

The men were sheiks, or so they liked to call themselves. Pinstriped suits and vests on some men who shouldn't even have worn a double-breasted coat. Their hair was flattened down by every kind of pomade except axle grease to give even blondes the Valentino look. Shoes sportif—à la Fred Astaire. In the summer the pinstripe gave way to the white, yellow, or off-white ice cream suit. Summer, too, was a good time for women to try out new hairstyles—inevitably bobbed or banged—and some went through as many colors of hair a month as they did shades of lipstick.

On weekends in the dance halls there was usually a cover charge, seldom during the week. Special drinks and special nights were invented to attract customers during the week. Some of the more popular girls and the best dancers were given a small retainer and allowed to keep half the dime or quarter their sheiks shelled out per dance. While Prohibition was still on, it was no problem. Usually the cops who worked the beat turned their heads when the flasks were brought out and most of the male customers had had a few— just a few—before arriving at the dance hall. While there were fights, they were less prevalent than today. The bouncers were big, and when a fight broke out at one end of the dance hall, they could eject a man so fast that by the time word reached the other side the disturbance was over and those involved were out on the street sobering up or on their way to the next dance palace.

For the time being, all the investigations had centered on Oakland. Since I was born there and spent the first two years of my life living there, it was the obvious jumping-off point.

Still with so many conflicting stories I knew it was entirely possible, if not altogether probable, that my father and mother had spent only the briefest time together. That meant he could indeed have been merely passing through Oakland on his way to anywhere. Suppose my mother didn't know his name but made one up instead? What if he had lied to her in the first place? Perhaps he was already married and didn't want any trouble. I decided that in all probability my father, whoever he was, had spent very little time in Oakland. And my chances of finding him there, far from expanding, had grown dimmer with each new discovery.

In December a Colorado newspaper staff was asked to submit names of friends and people they wanted to say Happy New Year to. When the list was published on January 1, it covered the entire front page and my name was on it. For a while Neilson & Green considered this a possible lead, since someone had misspelled my last name—God knows in which variation this time.

I have long had an affinity for Colorado, having worked there years ago as a cowboy, and for the past eight years, once or twice a year, I've appeared in concert in Denver, Red Rocks, or Colorado Springs. I have good friends in Denver and find it an easy and congenial city to bum around and get lost in. The Country and Western bars have the best selections on their jukeboxes this side of East Texas.

One day Florence Fischer, who had conducted a successful search for her missing father, called and offered help. She had known about my background for a long time and although we had never met we had corresponded and talked on the telephone. Dick Carlson had been in touch with her and told her that I had now intensified my lifelong campaign to find my dad. When I explained how little we had to go on she wasn't negative at all, just admitted the search would be more difficult.

One of my favorite songwriters, Peter Allen, sent a song to me entitled "Will We Ever Find Our Fathers?" The title scared me, but when I read the lyrics and listened to the music I liked it so much I recorded the song that day. Warner Bros., who release my records, refused to put it out, terming it "non-commercial." I still seize the chance to sing it anywhere, at concerts, to my friends—I like it enough to sing it on street corners, and recently performed it with the Cincinnati Symphony.

Some of my mother's effects were stored in the basement. I had not been able to bring myself to go through them since her death. As a matter of fact, I hadn't even answered sympathy cards or thanked the people who sent flowers and made donations to the Cancer Society. I had tried to put the moment off and, of course, I was really only delaying it until some future time when it would have a greater impact than if I'd dealt with the situation directly, honestly in the first place. Now, after four years, I reasoned that going through her private things wouldn't be all that difficult.

There were boxes of clothes that I finally sent off to the Salvation Army. Some hadn't even been worn, since they were bought as Christmas presents a few months before her death, and right after Christmas she began to lose so much weight that nothing really fit her. Ed and I knew how sick she was at the time, and I suppose because of that we were even more lavish than usual with our presents. It's strange how many things I came across that she probably never would have needed or used had she lived—but that last Christmas *had* to be filled with pretty things and frilly things we thought would cheer her up. I even bought her a mink coat, which she finally had to stop wearing to the hospital because it was too heavy. Soon after her death I gave it away to her friend Elsie.

Love somehow even takes precedence over ethics. It's a matter of principle and record that I would never date a girl who wears a fur coat, but Mama always wanted a mink. So she got one—even though it was too late.

Just before Christmas when I came back from London I'd brought her a diamond ring from Gerrards. I still have it for no good reason. There was a billfold half-filled with the pictures my brother had left with her of his various and sundry girlfriends; military service pictures of Billy and myself and a Bible belonging to my grandmother. In other boxes we had removed from her rooms, I found all the costume jewelry—not much of it any good—that Bill and Ed and I had given her over the years for birthdays, Christmases, and anniversaries. There were two full charm bracelets with charms from perhaps sixty or seventy cities I'd visited. Old photographs and cards and letters I'd sent her over the years were the only papers and letters I found.

I knew there were trunks and suitcases and boxes Mama had left in towns and had never gone back to pick up. We were always going to send for them, and every time we had money enough we forgot about it or just neglected to take the necessary action that might have left me with a little more of my mother than I have. The photographs I liked best of her are still the ones taken when she was a young girl. A special favorite shows her paddling a canoe with one of her brothers in some unnamed Oregon lake.

The final discovery at the bottom of a cardboard box stuffed with old handbags and shoes was a real surprise—a small notebook filled with thoughts and poetry written by my grandmother, Jesse Woolever. In her notebook/diary there were quotations from other poets (Byron seemed to be a favorite) and there were snatches of poems obviously her own, very plain thoughts that showed an intelligent use of language. The most interesting thing to me was that many of the sentiments she expressed were put down in nearly the same way in which I was later to write my own poetry.

Of course, nowhere in any of Mama's personal effects was there anything on my father. Absolutely nothing. Not that I thought there would be.

**Mama smiled a lot
but never once to anyone
she didn't care about
or wouldn't like to know.**

**When Mama frowned
you had to question her,
often and a lot
to find the reason why.**

We seldom ever did.

    I can't remember Mama ever having many close woman friends. Perhaps one or two in Las Vegas and the lady she worked with when we lived in Oakland when my brother and I were teen-agers. When the three of us were living in Los An-

geles on Gardner, there was a woman across the street my
mother saw a lot of. And once when Patsy Kelly lived upstairs
in the Gardner Street house, she and my mother became very
close. To suddenly come upon Claire Moseley and Irma
King—two women who claimed to have known my mother
during and just before the time of my birth—came as quite a
shock. There was to be a third.

Joy Orr was born Joy Green in February 1912 making
her a little more than two years younger than Mama who was
born in September of 1909. She was eighteen when she met
my mother. By the middle of 1930, Mrs. Orr worked as an
usherette in the Century Theatre in downtown Oakland. She
remembers that Mama was living at the Stanford Hotel on
San Pablo, and working as a waitress at the coffeeshop located
in the hotel. Mama went to work early and came home in the
afternoon and the two were constantly running into each other. Although Mrs. Orr said my mother liked music, she does
not remember her working as a taxi dancer, at least not during the time she knew her.

Joy Orr called the investigators in late December after
reading the classified ad in the *Chronicle*. At first she was hesi-
tant to identify my mother, but when she was shown photographs she said they had "jumped" out at her. She was absolutely positive that the woman in the photographs was the
same Clarice she knew more than forty years ago. She isn't
sure how they met, perhaps through mutual friends or her
own older brother, Leland, a regular customer of dance halls
in the East Bay Area.

"Somehow the two of us just seemed to hit it off right
from the start and we used to see each other on a regular and
frequent basis," Joy says. She would often take the streetcar
to visit Clarice at the Stanford Hotel, in the coffeeshop, the
hotel lobby, or her apartment.

Five and one-half hours of taped conversations with
Mrs. Orr reveal that very early on in their friendship she be-

came aware that Clarice was having a regular relationship with a man. Joy knew him only as Mack. That was one of the reasons the classified advertisement had startled her so, immediately suggesting that someone was looking for those two people she'd known so long ago.

Mrs. Orr had a clear recall of the man she knew as Mack. He was twenty-five or twenty-eight years old, 5'6" or 5'8" tall, and weighed about 150 pounds. He had a slight build and no noticeable scars or marks. His complexion was fair. He didn't wear glasses and was clean-cut—no beard, no mustache, no long sideburns—and was always immaculate in his appearance. Although she never remembered seeing him in a business suit, he was always nattily dressed in casual clothes, right down to his shoes, which were perpetually polished. His hair was light brown and combed straight back, which was the style.

Would he approve of me, blue-jeaned, bearded, and sneakered?

Mrs. Orr doesn't recall the man's last name but she's sure that Mama referred to him often as Mack. She was also pretty sure the two were very much in love. "Clarice was always very attentive to Mack." On the occasions when Mrs. Orr came in contact with Mack, she remembered that Clarice seemed anxious to please and to be with him. They enjoyed each other's company and liked to spend a lot of time together. Maybe for this reason, or because they didn't have a great deal in the way of material things, they didn't go out very much. Mack had his own key and kept some of his clothes at the Stanford apartment. To all intents and purposes, he was living with my mother. Although Mrs. Orr doesn't know how Clarice and Mack were registered at the Stanford Hotel, it was clear in a conversation my mother had with her that they were not married. However, as far as everyone else was concerned, they were husband and wife.

* * *

**The hotel room is four flights up
just high enough for me to see
the tops of heads I'll never touch.
Brown hair, yellow hair,
hatless heads and heads with hats.
People alone, people together
watched by my sniper's eye—
poised to drop invisible love bombs.**

Mrs. Orr maintains she never heard the name McKuien/McKuen in any variation of spelling; she also doesn't think the two were using Woolever as a last name while passing themselves off as a married couple. She doesn't remember anything about how Mack made his living. He might have been a salesman. She does remember that he had an older model car but she cannot describe it except that it was big.

Joy recalls that while Mack was always cordial to her, they had never had any long conversations. If she was visiting Clarice when Mack stopped by, she would find some pretext to leave. It was basically her feeling that "two's company, three's a crowd."

Although she considered my mother a loner, she evidently didn't think of her as unfriendly. Clarice got along fine with her co-workers in the coffeeshop but never volunteered much information about her personal life. And Joy Orr never pressed her.

A month and a day before I was born, Joy Orr left the Bay Area. She never saw Clarice or Mack again. But she had known the two of them well enough during that period to help a police artist make a drawing of Mack for this investigation. She said she was reasonably satisfied that the drawing made by Inspector Holbert Nelson resembled the "type" of man she remembered Mack to be.

In summing up his report on Joy Orr, after listening to the hours of tape recordings and meeting her, Detective

Green concluded, "Mrs. Orr is a very careful and conscientious lady. Her memory is apparently excellent about many things that happened so long ago. When she can not remember something she says so without hesitation. We see no reason to disbelieve her."

Claire Moseley and Irma King, questioned again in the light of this new information, didn't remember Mrs. Orr. But Mrs. King again recalled the first two years *after* I was born—the remaining years of the Depression: "When Rod was about two years old, Clarice disappeared altogether, eventually winding up in Nevada. Fern was trying to find her and she was up in Nevada so she knew where she went. She sent the police up there and she [Clarice] was living in a motel and had then married the man [Hooper] and then came back and took Rodney. That's when she did the disappearing act."

There are some forests that I haven't known.
Some tree trunks I've never wrapped my legs
around

and climbed.
A million branches I might have slid down
had I had the time.

Still
some leaves trembled in the wood and caught
my ear.
Some twigs beneath the hooves of deer snapped
and signaled spring
waking me from endless winter thoughts.

By January 15, 1976, I had received but hardly been
able to read or digest, nearly two thousand pieces of mail.

173

More would come. There were phone calls made to my office. Letters sent to broadcasting companies, to my home, to my office, to publications that had interviewed me, and to my publisher's address which eventually found their way to me. Add the daily calls and letters that Neilson & Green received, checking some out, forwarding others to me.

I was now only halfway through digesting the investigator's preliminary report with all its exhibits and photographs. Somehow I managed to put in a full day's work every day, but foremost in my mind was that at any minute the telephone or the doorbell would ring and he would be there. My father. I never doubted it for a minute. And at the end of each new lead, when all I was left with was hope, hope was always enough.

In the process of living and getting on with it, acquaintances and friends pass in and out of our lives without our missing them or sometimes even being aware they've gone. People are misplaced or forgotten not because we want them to be, but because with each receding and succeeding day the hours get smaller and there is so much more to be learned—so many more things to do. Alas, those people we wish to forget are remembered because we allow them too much time in our thoughts, trying to forget them.

As far back as I can remember, I remember Mama's friends Hilda and Jean Nielson. They were just about the only friends she had from years past that she bothered to keep in touch with. Mama always referred to the two sisters affectionately as "the Mormons," forgetting, I suppose, that her husband Bill and his family had been Mormons and that I, too, had been baptized a Mormon when I was eight years old. Still, the "the Mormons" was the special collective name reserved for Hilda and Jean Nielson.

Today they live with their brother Leo in Southern California. I hadn't seen Hilda since my mother's funeral. Sometime before that, Jean came to visit my mother when she was ill. Both women went to school with Mama in Union,

Oregon. Later they knew each other in Oakland when Mama had moved there.

In 1959, when I was under contract to Universal Studios, I had a steady job and the money to move my mother and Billy down to Los Angeles. I was living in a two-story white house on the corner of Gardner and Fountain. It stands there still. The elephant ears and the cypress trees I planted have grown up to totally screen the porch. Part of the property is cut back because Fountain was later widened into a near-boulevard—the bulldozers taking a row of old trees on either side of the street. If I am within blocks of the area, I pass the house on purpose. It looks the same to me. I often have the urge to knock on the door and find out who's living there now. Though I never have.

Before I left Oakland and went into the Army I had a large collection of 78 rpm records. Having worked as a disc jockey at a radio station, I was on the mailing list of every record company, and even then, whenever I had pocket money, I preferred to spend it on a book or a record, not a beefsteak. While I was in Korea, my mother had had to move to a smaller house in Oakland and was unable to take my record collection with her. So in the Gardner Street house I began to assemble and build a new collection of records that now numbers in the thousands. It's probably my biggest extravagance, and I now have a real record room as opposed to that hallway back on Gardner.

Still, many of my best songs and some of the poems that seem to have lasted over the years were written as I lay stretched out on the floor in that hallway, reading or listening to music. I had a desperate crush on Sally Kellerman, then a struggling singer, and I used to see her often. Our best times were spent listening to records of obscure singers, uncovering neglected songs by important and unimportant writers. Some of those songs now form the basis of Sally's current act and many inspired me and pushed me along in writing my own music and lyrics.

When Mom first came down to Los Angeles, she and Billy lived in an apartment attached to my house. She had so much concern for my privacy that she never came over without calling first—something even some friends won't do. I can honestly say that I never remember my mother opening a letter addressed to me. Not ever. When I finally came home to Gardner Street from New York my preoccupation was still songwriting. It was at the height of the "folk" craze, and Mom found herself acting as cook and sounding board for all manner of performers—among them Glenn Yarbrough, Barry McGuire, Gale Garnett, Alex Gottlieb, Jimmie Rodgers, Bob Shane of the Kingston Trio, Ramblin' Jack Elliott (who was then part of a folk group I had started), Travis Edmondson, Tommy Sands, Tommy Leonetti, Eddy Arnold, and an unemployed songwriter named Jimmy Webb.

The house was home to or a stopping place for a number of actors, too. Some were left over from my Universal days and others were just friends who'd drop by, and if I wasn't there they knew they could go next door and rustle up my mother for a chat or a bowl of soup: Sally, Nick Adams, Joan Collins, Theo Bikel, Peter Palmer, Roger Miller, Terry Moore and Peter Ford, Clint Eastwood, Kim Novak, Sal Mineo, Carleton Carpenter (who, by the way, writes great songs), and Ronnie Burns. Herb Alpert and Jerry Moss, who were just starting A & M Records, used to stop by. Years later they ended up with a catalogue of some of my best songs in their publishing company.

While I was still at Universal I'd introduced Mom to Montgomery Clift. One night I arrived home late from the studio and found her, Patsy Kelly, and Monty in a rather advanced stage of inebriation. Monty was passed out on the couch, Patsy was cracking open some ice from the refrigerator, and Mom, weaving and wavering, was sitting in the living room playing a slower than usual game of solitaire.

Hilda and Jean Nielson used to visit us on Gardner Street. Always there was the nostalgia talk. I called them again this spring. They said an investigator had phoned after tracing them from Union. I assured them he was authorized, liking the protective tone they took toward me. They told me in essence what they had told the detective. My mother had gone with this McKuen man for some time. One night he assaulted her in the Oakland Hotel. At that time Jean was working across the street at Valentine's Restaurant. My mother had gotten pregnant and the man had wanted to marry her but my mother would have nothing to do with him. What did he look like? "He was tall, more than six feet, blond, and a reporter for the Oakland *Tribune*." Not a refrigerator salesman? "No." Not a demonstrator of sheet music? "No, a reporter for the Oakland *Tribune*." Where had he lived? "At the Oakland Hotel." In rechecking the Oakland telephone directories of 1932, Green discovered a J. McKoen; his address: the Oakland Hotel. Now it remained for Green's investigator to check with the *Tribune* to discover whether or not a McKoen had worked there during the thirties.

The investigators had come across another interesting lead. In looking through a 1923 Los Angeles City Directory, they had uncovered a Rodney Marion McKune. Considering my mother named me Rodney Marvin McKuen, it held a lot of significance. I'd always wondered why my mother had chosen such an odd first and middle name. And, of course, I'd assumed I must have been named after my father, who probably, like me, didn't much care for the first name Rodney.

Usually there's a good reason for giving a child a particular name. It might be a favorite uncle or a grandparent's name. If it's a girl, and the father had his heart set on a boy to name after his father, Joe, she might end up being called Joanne, or in the Southern United States where they invent such beautiful first names, she might be given a compromise—Joline, Jody, or Joemae. During the height of the Presley mania, hundreds of children were probably christened Elvis. And it would be interesting to know how many subteens today have the moniker John, Paul, George, or Ringo.

Rod McKuen.

Although my mother was a great Crosby fan, fortunately I wasn't named Bing—a tough act to follow. The only first name I can come up with that might be taken from a personality popular at that time was Rod La Roque. The only Marvin I know of, who I think was big even in the 1930s, was Marvin Gardens in Monopoly. At any rate, I don't think I was named after a movie star and a piece of paper property, so here was a name eerily close to mine. My mother could have made a mistake on the Marion part or at least decided Marvin was close enough. I eagerly awaited further news of Rodney Marion McKune.

In addition to our initial phone calls, an investigator had paid a personal visit to Hilda and Jean on February 10, 1976, in Los Angeles. The two sisters were interviewed for several hours. According to them, when Clarice was about twelve, the Woolever family moved away from Union, causing a gap in their friendships until the early 1930s when they met again in Oakland. While Hilda had also known Clarice, her contacts were mostly with Fern.

One event helpful in establishing a time frame was the death of their own older sister, who died in Oakland while on a visit from Oregon in July, 1932. Jean said that when her sister died, she had been living in California for some years and, while she could not recall the precise way she'd run into Clarice again, she was certain it was well before her sister's death.

Jean's best recollection was that she met Clarice again sometime in 1931. Jean was working as a waitress at Valentine's Restaurant across the street from the Oakland Hotel. When Jean and Clarice were reunited, they immediately hit it off again and became fast friends. They both loved to dance and often went out together to dance halls like Sweet's Ballroom. Later on, Clarice took a job as a taxi dancer at one of the dime-a-dance places in downtown Oakland. When pressed as to which one, Jean said the Rose Room and/or Danceland sounded right, but she was not positive.

Jean worked the late shift at Valentine's and Clarice often came into the restaurant after work, sometimes accompanied by different men friends she'd evidently met while working as a taxi dancer. Jean emphasized that Clarice was primarily after something to eat and was not with these men for any other reason. She could not recall that Clarice had any particular favorite or steady boyfriend at the time. When the two of them went out together, they invariably went by themselves. Occasionally they would meet men at the halls, but rarely did they leave with anyone they met casually. In fact, Jean recalled only one time when they allowed themselves to be given a ride home by a couple of men, and she insisted that nothing ever came of it. I'm inclined to believe this, because while Jean could not be considered a prude by anybody's definition, her religious beliefs have always seemed stronger than her sexual appetite, and regardless of what my mother's desires might have been, Jean's will would probably have prevailed.

Jean was certain that throughout that first year, Clarice was living at the Abbey Apartments. She recalled that Clarice shared a basement apartment with Fern while Ruth and her two boys lived in a nearby apartment on the same floor. (Note: This is significant because that was the same period Joy Orr maintains that Clarice was working as a waitress at the Stanford Hotel and living with "Mac.")

Was *everybody* right? Jean, Joy Orr, and Mrs. Moseley? Maybe Mama *was* leading some kind of double life. God knows the pressure from her two older sisters to bring home the bacon could have caused her to seek relief somewhere. If not in a stranger's arms, perhaps she shared a second apartment with a friend. The possibilities were becoming so endless that anything was possible and everything was probable.

Jean did not recollect ever hearing Clarice mention the

Stanford Hotel or "Mac." As far as she could recall, Clarice lived at the Abbey Apartments until Fern and Clarice moved into an apartment on Madison Avenue.

Jean and Hilda were shown photographs of the Abbey Apartments and both confirmed it was the building where the Woolever sisters were living in 1932. They also remembered that Fern had already started her bootlegging business. Although Jean was a close friend of Clarice, she did not learn that Clarice was pregnant until after Rod was born. At this point both sisters recognized an inconsistency and discussed where they had been during late 1932 and early 1933. They then remembered that after their sister died in July, 1932, they both had gone to Oregon for a while, so they were not in Oakland the balance of the year. In June, 1934, their ailing mother died in Oregon and Hilda had spent additional time with her before her death.

Jean recognized the photograph of the apartment building at 1109 Madison Avenue. This was where she had first seen little Rodney. In fact, Jean herself subsequently moved into a second-floor apartment in the same building in order to be close to her friends.

There was also some confusion in Jean's mind regarding who gave her what details about how Clarice became pregnant. Jean was convinced Clarice had told her something about her pregnancy, but she also believed she had heard most of the details from Ruth and Fern. It hadn't been a topic the Woolever sisters were especially eager to discuss.

Jean's basic recollection was that Clarice had been raped. The man responsible was someone Clarice did not know well and whom she apparently did not love. Somehow Clarice had found herself locked in a hotel room with this man, who either beat her and/or got her drunk in order to have sexual relations with her.

I still couldn't picture Mama being raped. She had a boyfriend once when she was out of work and we were living in Oakland, after she and Billy had rejoined me. He was clearly being strung along by Mom in order to provide us with an occasional meal. One Thanksgiving he threatened to take his turkey and go home if Mama continued to resist his advances. I'll never forget her handing him the half-stuffed bird and telling him to get out. He did.

Jean added that the man Clarice had been "assaulted" by had reportedly wanted to marry her and that he was a man of some means, but that Mama wanted no part of him. Well, that was Mama all right. She could be indifferent even if it cost Thanksgiving dinner.

Jean believed the assault took place in the Oakland Hotel on 14th Street across from Valentine's. Asked if it could have been the Olympic Hotel or the Alpine Hotel, Jean replied that neither sounded right. She had never heard how Clarice met the man.

Hilda and Jean thought Clarice had referred to my father as a newspaperman, but if so, she could not recall which paper he had worked for. They were shown my birth certificate, stating that the father was a refrigerator salesman but had no recollection of anyone telling them such a thing. Jean described my father as perhaps thirty years of age, possibly younger, between 5'9" and 6' tall, of medium build, and with blondish hair.

While all the "eyewitnesses" seemed to ascribe different addresses and locations where Mama was living, and to have only a hazy sense of my father as to job and origin, their physical description of him is fairly uniform. He is consistently pictured as around six feet tall, of medium build and light complected. Of course, that description fits me perfectly. Maybe without knowing it, the witnesses were basing their description on what Rod McKuen appeared to be and not on the "Mac" McKuen of forty years before. There was no way of determining that.

Asked if she had ever seen Clarice and this man together, Jean replied that she had not. Asked what had caused her to single him out as the father, she replied that he was in the newspaper business, was seen in the area, and that she had always believed he was the man.

Jean and Hilda were then shown some of the photographs and the composite drawing but were not given any information about them. Jean was immediately interested in the composite drawing and said it had some similarities to the man she thought was the father. The drawing was too general and Jean's memory too vague for any positive identification. But she said she thought the drawing looked like Rod McKuen!

Jean confessed she had always been bothered by the rape story. She found it very hard to understand how Clarice ever could have got herself in a position to be raped. She had never considered that Clarice had loose morals or was free with her favors. In fact, she thought it was quite possible the rape story was a fabrication.

Jean and Hilda both studied the Rose Room photograph, but did not recognize anyone.

In the course of the interview the sisters were shown photographs of Rodney Marion McKune—photographs I had not yet seen. They didn't recognize the man in the pictures. And that seemed to be that.

Jean had continued her friendship with Clarice until Clarice left for Nevada. They'd kept in touch with each other over the years, but not on a regular basis until they all came together in Southern California. Hilda went to Clarice's funeral, but Jean had been unable to attend because of her job.

Who was my mother? Even after twenty or thirty years have passed it seems she was a totally different human being to each person who allegedly remembers her, yet each description is so graphic that they *all* seem true. Maybe I never gave my mother credit for being the complex individual she must have been. And if I knew so much about her and still had so little to go on about my father, did he exist? Does he move about me somewhere never to be known or stumbled upon? Certainly people who don't know me consider me very complex. Even friends, when interviewed by the press, say they don't really know me—or that at best I'm three or four people trying to get out of one. Sometimes the most discouraging thing about the letters I get is that while there are those who say I fulfill a certain need for them, I end up being so different and my work accepted and rejected in so many different ways and for such a variety of reasons no definitive portrait of me can be drawn. Parts of the opera I've written, *The Black Eagle,* have become even more autobiographical than my poetry. The following lyrics to an aria from it entitled "The Stone Song" are as close as I've come to describing the frustration I feel about myself and my life.

> **Some people run from me,**
> **some people flee from me,**
> **some people see me in only themselves.**
> **Others there are who are bent on believing me**
> **only the way that they want me to be.**
>
> **If I knew why I was who it is that I am**
> **or, who I ought to be I'd be a kinder man,**
> **but as it is I am all things to everyone**
> **ending up being *nothing* to anyone.**
>
> **Even to me I'm less than I want to be.**
> **More of myself has been lost as I've grown.**
> **Who was I anyway? Nothing in any way**
> **that would resemble a semblance of *own*.**

**Help me. I need to be, helped into being me,
though I'm a simple stone,
I can't stand alone.**

As the reports came in, in bunches, paragraphs, whole transcripts on tape, and on paper from the people on these pages—and some I haven't even quoted who claim to have known my mother and father—I was not so much seized by a sense of frustration as I was by the feeling that I was experiencing my own private *Rashomon*. How could I hope to unravel anything? Indeed, what was the point, if any, of continuing with the investigation? Oakland and that old life, whatever it was, was a long time ago and maybe by now there wasn't any real truth to be found.

Lie down and leave your imprint in the sand,
my hand will trace it into everything I need.
That's how reality begins,
    shadows made into something real
or reality turned back into a shadow.
I need the sureness of the shadow world again.
To make me whole.

If I am anything at all
I'm what I've gotten out of sand.
Not only that washed in
    from seas and islands
but any piece of earth
    (however small)
a man can hold
securely in his hand.

Rod McKuen

I went back to Oakland a year ago and visited the last house I'd lived in there. The occasion for returning to the city was to receive my high school diploma twenty years late and to give an assembly for the students as a way of saying thank you. I had a little time before my flight back to Southern California so I drove my rented car to the old corner on 17th Street I remembered so well.

Instead of the Mom-and-Pop store operation underneath the apartment there was now a laundromat. On the front of the door leading upstairs was a "For Rent" sign. I couldn't resist ringing the doorbell, which brought the manager of the laundromat and the new owner of the property to the door. I asked to see the flat upstairs and was promptly shown in.

The apartment had a new coat of paint. The rent was pretty close to what it had been back in the early fifties, and as I looked out the window a flood of memories came back. Most of all I remembered that house at 645 17th Street as being the first place where I had my own room. I had nailed up orange crates from floor to ceiling around the walls and used them as a record and book library. In that room I read my first novels, *The Naked and the Dead, You Can't Go Home Again,* and Truman Capote's early works, especially *Other Voices, Other Rooms,* and it was also there that I began to be interested in books and music of all kinds. My favorite American authors became Hemingway, Isherwood, Sandburg, Whitman, Dickinson, and just about any author whose body of work seemed to me immediate and uncluttered. I started out liking so-called middle-of-the-road music, then moved through jazz, and began to have a good rapport with the classics. Thankfully, over the years my tastes haven't settled on any one area of music.

Uncle Ted, without knowing it, was responsible for expanding many of my horizons. A great, robust man, overweight and smiling, he used to come back from his voyages

186

with fantastic stories. I guess in his lifetime as a seaman Ted had been everywhere—the South Seas, the North Atlantic—and it was my uncle's encouragement and the excitement his tales generated that made me want to leave the confines of the room on 17th Street and seek a larger world.

After they'd visited for a while Ted and my mother would drink pints, then quarts, of Corby's whiskey. (Billy and I could determine how much they'd had to drink by how many parrots they'd saved for us—the whiskey used to come with a plastic parrot on a chain taped to each bottleneck.) They'd talk about the old times back in San Francisco and in Union, but I never remember hearing them speak about my father, and I never asked.

Uncle Ted and Mom would get very drunk sometimes and Ted would begin to spin endless rambling sea stories. I think he was afraid to go home to his wife in San Francisco, a no-nonsense woman who didn't put up with his drinking. Years later I was playing the Fairmont in San Francisco, and Ted and Frieda and their neighbors came to see me. Ted had given up drinking and I was both happy and sad—happy because I was sure his domestic life was in good shape now, and sad because Ted loved to drink. People should be allowed, within reason, to do the things they love to do. But I can't deny that it was nice to see a man who felt the woman he loved was more important than a habit that might drive her from him.

Ted wrote me yesterday and asked how the search was coming. "We've tried to help the investigators in every way we know how," he stated, "and I hope you find your father. I think I hope most of all that you'll never forget what a wonderful woman your mother was." I haven't answered Ted's letter. I don't think I have to.

Having seen all the reports from Neilson & Green and having talked to friends of my mother, some I never knew about until this new chapter of my quest began, I'm aware of a kind of whitewash job done on my Mama's character. By that I don't mean to imply that she was anything but the best lady I ever knew. But it would be doing her a terrible disservice to include the reports and conversations here without some kind of balance.

I don't think my mother was capable of meanness, although she certainly was able to get mad, even though very infrequently and never for long. Mom had always had a good capacity for liquor, though I'm not quite sure when she became a "secret drinker." It probably started sometime after she left Las Vegas and moved back to Oakland. Not at first, because in the beginning she still worked as a bartender (somehow I hate to use the word "barmaid," for while she was easily as liberated as anyone I've ever met, she was definitely not a "bar person"). It must have been while Billy and I were growing up. As I said before, she didn't have many women friends, and despite our urging we couldn't get her to go out with anyone. She just wasn't interested. Later, in Los Angeles, after Mom virtually adopted Ed, he too tried to fix her up with various eligible bachelors. By now Mom was not only not interested, but could be downright rude if she suspected a setup—which she always did.

Mom had begun drinking wine and that bothered me. She knew it and would use all manner of disguises and hiding places to prevent confirming my suspicions. She was really ingenious in her methods; most often the liquor would be in some very ordinary place where none of us would think to look for it. At some point she switched to vodka, and Ed and I used to water that down until she caught us at it.

If Mom was lonely it was a self-imposed loneliness. She was shy and yet very quick to warm up to my friends—the ones she approved of. As my work became more recognized and I became a more public person, she took on a new responsibility, cautioning me and attempting to weed out the fair-weather from my newfound friends. She was unerring in her instinct for pretension and phoniness. On the other hand, I could have been sold the Brooklyn Bridge and probably was a time or two, though not within her earshot.

No doubt about it, Mom was alone a lot of the time. For company she really preferred to be with Bill, Ed, or myself. Of course, that got more and more difficult as we grew up. I was usually going in several directions at once, never sure what I wanted to do with my life—and not all that sure now.

Ed was in and out, here and gone, caring and careless.

My brother Bill really wanted to go his own way, and once I was more or less settled in Los Angeles, he began to do the kind of traveling and working at odd jobs that I had gotten out of my system as a teen-ager. Unlike me, for some reason Bill usually had friends who tended to be younger than he was, and some of the less mature ones even attempted to lead him into trouble. None of us has had much difficulty being led along *that* route, but amazingly we've each been able to extricate ourselves from difficult situations.

Mama was left alone.

I wish I'd known some formula for making my mother less alone or some way any of us could have offered more comfort to her than we did. God knows we loved her. Sometimes even love isn't enough. Mom was never falling-down drunk or hospitalized as a chronic alcoholic or even an embarrassment to me if she had been drinking and a friend dropped by—she was just a quiet drinker. She drank too much. After a while the three of us decided Mom seemed to have so little enjoyment in life that if she liked drinking then that was fine with us. It wasn't an easy decision or an easy out; for better or for worse, I still believe it was sensible on our part and if any of us had it to do again, we would make the same decision.

Drinking usually goes with violence, and I can't stand violence in any form; there was so much of it around me when I was a kid that I have no ability left to tolerate it. My mother's sister, Fern, could be quite caustic when she was sober, but really mean and full of recrimination when she'd had a few drinks. Uncle Ted was a noisy drunk but a kind man—I wouldn't, however, have liked him as an adversary on a Hong Kong dockside after he'd put away a half case of beer. Mama drank all right, but she was never mean or violent because of it. And the only time she became morose or unhappy was when one of us found out and reproached her for it. As each of us ultimately got smart enough to realize this, we all stopped criticizing her.

On April 12, 1971, Mama died of a kind of cancer not known in women till they started smoking heavily. She didn't die from drinking. Yet, as well as Bill and Ed and I knew Mom, I wouldn't be at all surprised if there was some method of learning it, that she had hidden within her a kind of heartbreak or emptiness none of us sensed while she was alive. I suppose yet another reason why I've never considered myself a "proper" bastard is because I can never imagine my mother capable of an act of immorality. While times have changed and morals with them, in 1933 or 1935 it must have been considered immoral indeed to mother a child without being married. I'm glad about that aspect of change in our mores. I only wish it had come about soon enough to have kept my mother from feeling guilty, if she ever did.

I'm not sure when I started to realize how much Joan Blondell reminded and reminds me of my mother. They never knew each other and I don't think I ever discussed Joan with Mom, other than to say that I was a genuine fan. As I recall, with that bit of news my mother ticked off a number of Joan's early films I hadn't yet come across.

Even though Joanie and I are good friends now, I've never mentioned that there's a certain aura about her that always brings my mother to me vividly and true. But in speaking about it with other friends who knew both women, I find they understand and concur with my feelings. I think it was Joan Blondell's vulnerability and her way of always coming out on top in the movies she appeared in, no matter how bad things seemed to get. By now I must have seen all of her films and the amount of admissions I spent on *Nightmare Alley* alone should have paid for several prints.

Mama and Joanie looked a great deal alike in the early pictures I have and in later years they both seemed to have matured in the same beautiful way. But it wasn't just the looks or the vulnerability or the ability always to come out on top— there was something else. Mama always seemed to be about to say something, but not really. There was always more in what she *didn't* say in a conversation than what actually came out. Joan Blondell, in person and as an actress, is very much like that. I wish they had met. Patsy Kelly said they would have been chums, "good chums."

Last Christmas Eve Joanie came for dinner. It was my first Christmas at home in a couple of years, and as usual I wanted to spend it with people I really care about. The guest list included Phyllis Diller, Joyce Haber, Jane Withers, Wade, my conductor Skip Redwine, Paul and Helen Janssen, Ed, Larry Phillips, and, of course, Joan. Many times during the evening I found myself looking at Joan—every bit a loner— losing all awareness of the conversation that was going on, and thinking of Mom.

I could just *see* my mother slinking by and charming that "sheik" who was to be my father. I'll bet they were *both* loners, both independent and maybe that's the reason they didn't or couldn't stay together. Certainly I'm like my mother in many ways, but I think it would have taken two loners to produce a son whose worn sneakers have taken him everywhere there is to go and who still goes on following strange streets in alien cities with no real destination in mind.

Rod McKuen

Sometimes I can see the paper Japanese lanterns that must have caught my mother's smile as she passed by that lonesome wanderer. So much magic and illusion comes when people are on the move, not settled—when the light's just right, when the lack of any real purpose in life makes the only purpose the need for one other human being.

There is no single day
                or time
within the life
I've so far lived
that I'd have changed
                or altered.

Possibly there are some days
I could have missed
and never missed,
but I suspect that I could not
have come down to this place
                a different way.
As I suspect that being here
I don't as yet know where I am.

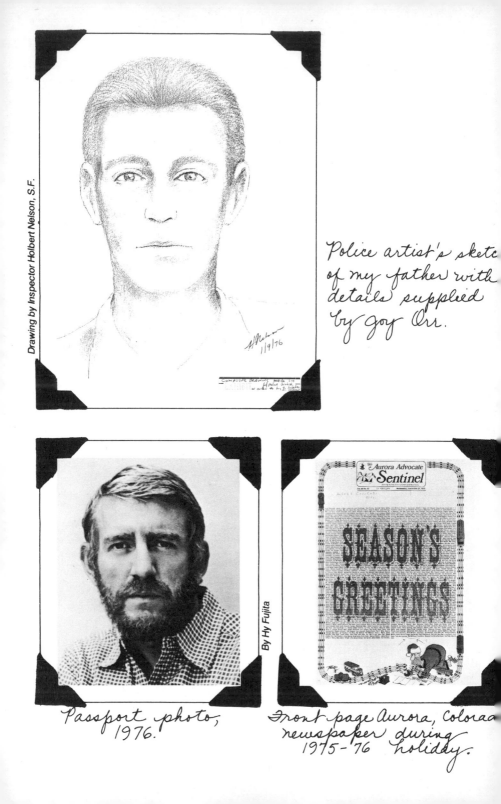

Drawing by Inspector Holbert Nelson, S.F.

Police artist's sketch of my father with details supplied by Joy Orr.

By Hy Fujita

Passport photo, 1976.

Front page Aurora, Colorado newspaper during 1975-76 holiday.

I cannot speculate
on what the cluttered mind
will finally save,
    sleepy Sundays
or a nosebleed after love.

I only know the dying heart
needs the nourishment of memory
to live beyond too many winters.

Michael Hamel-Green is a former member of British
Intelligence. He came to the U.S.A. in 1952 and worked for a
while at Trans-World Airlines. His next-door neighbor in the
apartment building he was living in was working as a private
investigator. He suggested that Green, with his background,
would not only make a good detective but could certainly

earn far more than his salary with the airline. At first Green was doubtful, but he finally went to work for an agency and in a short time became their chief investigator. Later he was a partner in the firm, Neilson & Green. In 1960 he bought Neilson out but retained the agency name.

Green is an affable Englishman who employs a staff of private investigators whose specialty is investigative work for corporate business. One of his most ambitious projects was done as a labor of love—an investigative report on the prevention of cruelty to animals. It's thorough and incisive. Completed in September of 1971, it triggered similar actions by concerned animal lovers all over America. One of the latest is the courageous battle waged by actress Gretchen Wyler against the National SPCA in New York City, an organization that Ms. Wyler contends does not have a single officer on its board of directors who is a member of any other animal organization.

Much of the writing on the Neilson & Green animal report was done by Green. His writing is thoughtful, and lets the facts present themselves. He used the same technique in pulling together his reports for me. I've alluded to Green's reports before and in some cases quoted the transcripts directly, but it is difficult to get across to the reader unless he sees it for himself just how comprehensive Green's dossier on the matter of Mack McKuien is. Seldom does he conduct only a single interview with a subject unless he reaches a blank wall the first time out. Even then, if another source offers information he thinks the first might elaborate on, he or his investigators will return for a second or third go-round. In the case of his report for me, as many as five or six different interviews were held with a single eyewitness or someone Green felt could be of help.

At least thirty-five leads were tracked down in the first month of the investigation. Most ended nowhere. But at the

196

time of his preliminary report there were twelve active leads he and his investigators were checking.

Example: Rodney Marion McKune had lived in Utah. Green was in touch with the Church of Jesus Christ of Latter Day Saints' Genealogical Library in Salt Lake City, checking not only McKune but all the spellings of the name he had encountered. The Mormon Church hierarchy and their files are almost a city within Salt Lake City. While many of the old files have not been brought up to date, the newer entries are indexed and cross-filed by computer. Into the computer is fed genealogical information on hundreds of thousands of members of LDS, making their library one of the best anywhere in the world.

Next he asked the help of the U.S. General Service Administration's National Archives in San Bruno for information from the 1930 census.

The different people claiming to have known my mother have listed her residence variously as the Stanford Hotel, Abbey Apartments, Olympic Hotel, Alpine Hotel, and 4434 Penniman Avenue in Oakland. The Olympic Hotel has been torn down, but Green has a photograph of the site and uncovered an older shot showing the hotel itself. These, and photographs of the other hotels, together with the Rose Room, the Salvation Army maternity home, and the former site of Sherman Clay & Company have been circulated to all those who claim any knowledge of my mother. Always they were mixed in with other photographs so the witnesses would have to struggle with their memory in order to be sure. Green and his investigators also circulated a 1928 map of Oakland with all the sites mentioned marked on an enlarged sector.

Kelt's 1932 Geographical Directory of Oakland and the East Bay Cities, which listed street addresses, had various spellings of my name, but none of them helped.

The building at 1109 Madison Avenue in Oakland is a

three-story apartment. It was there that my Aunt Fern allegedly ran her bootlegging business. Yet no one living at that address now remembers the sisters. A check of telephone directories of the thirties shows no listings at all for that address; not that any of us expected there to be a listed number for "Fern's Bootlegging and Curio Operation."

If my mother or her sisters lived at the Abbey Apartments at 100 9th Street, now known as the Madison Park Apartments, none of them had telephones. That wasn't unusual since despite the fact that it is a very large apartment building, there were only nine listings in the 1932 directory, none of which any of the witnesses could identify. During *that* Depression it is not likely that home telephones were as common as they are in *this one.*

As I write this, photographs of Rodney Marion McKune are finally on their way to me to see if I think, as Green and some of the witnesses do, that there is a marked resemblance between us.

Although the services of a private investigator are extremely expensive, Green doesn't seem to be wasting the money. While the investigation was in progress, I saw the Roman Polanski film *Chinatown* again and barely managed to laugh when the private detective played by Jack Nicholson announced that his fee was $35 a day plus expenses. If only my investigation had started thirty years earlier.

I hadn't seen my brother Billy for nearly three years. That wasn't unusual since there have always been long separations in our lives, when we were growing up and after we became adults. I was aware that he was living somewhere in the vicinity of Portland and I hoped I would be able to track him down when I left last fall on a projected tour that included both Portland and Seattle. Not only had I begun to wonder about how he was getting along, but I welcomed the chance to see him and find out what new direction his life had taken.

Billy has been mixed up in as many different professions as I have and I never quite know what to expect when he reappears after a long absence.

Then, too, I knew he could be of great help in the investigation I was conducting. His memory has always been far better than mine and he was with my mother during the four years I spent away from home. She might easily have told him something about my original father that wasn't passed along to me.

When I did reach him he said that he had asked Mama many times about my father but with very little result. He did add some information. Among the things he told me was that he and Mom had once been riding a bus when they passed the Alpine Hotel and my mother said she used to work there as a waitress. It's Billy's impression that she had worked at the Alpine for a year or more. He even remembers her saying she had really enjoyed the people she worked for. He doesn't remember her mentioning Margaret Stewart, but I do and so does his father.

Billy was estranged from his own dad when my mother left Las Vegas to come to Oakland again in 1949. He didn't see him for a long time, but like me felt the need to go back and reacquaint himself with Bill Hooper. Using only his own detective work, he was able to do so in 1962. In the process he discovered a new family. My brother's search and reunion with his father gave us a far closer tie than we'd had in years.

Suddenly no matter where I looked, or even when I wasn't looking, I became intensely aware of an almost *universal search* that was going on. A young actor called to tell me the disastrous results he had when he discovered his long-lost mother and the terrible effects it continued to have on his psyche. Every time I picked up a paper I expected to be confronted by yet another long-lost family who suddenly got together again after many years of searching and soul-searching.

It must have been reported somewhere that I was running some kind of an agency to help relatives find one another. I began to get calls and letters from people who wanted me to help find sons, daughters, mothers, aunts, and fathers. I think somehow reports of my own search and of a foundation I long ago started (Animal Concern) became confused. It is certainly much easier for me to find parents for homeless animals than to find homes for lost parents. I finally had to develop a form letter to send back to people who couldn't understand why, if I was active in searching for my own father, I couldn't take a little time to help them find their missing loved ones.

Without exception people I would encounter were compassionate and solicitous. A friend I hadn't seen, a casual acquaintance, or someone recognizing me on the street would greet me, "Have you found your father yet?" I began to use the same sentence response to each and all who asked, "No, but I think we're close."

If I seemed dejected at times over the leads that went nowhere, and the information that turned out to be misinformation, I was more often than not buoyed by the fact that at last I was again actively working at finding my father. I was always sure it was only a matter of time. One morning I picked up a newspaper to find Ann Landers answering a question from someone who had written to her wondering why Miss Landers continued to advocate that adopted children not try to find their parents when "Rod McKuen had even hired a private detective to track down his father."

That same night my name was dropped on *Mary Hartman, Mary Hartman* (shortly afterward, the plot took a turn when Mary's mother discovered she was adopted and began searching for *her* father). *Phyllis,* on another channel, wondered why a new boyfriend left, since she "even sent him an autographed picture of Rod McKuen holding a cat." (Apparently even Norman Lear and Mary Tyler Moore were tuned in to my plight.) Surely my father was out there somewhere. If so, he must be finding it difficult to be unaware of his offspring.

Whatever I was to find, I was ready for it. I knew there might be pain and even unhappiness should I discover that my father was a man I couldn't relate to or one who didn't want to have anything to do with me; but I was sure in my own mind that no possible outcome could equal the unhappiness I'd known over the years in *not* knowing.

> I know love
> by its first name
> and living by its last.
> I'm not afraid
> of what's upcoming
> or what has gone before
> and if there's nothing left
> to know about or learn
> I'll review the early lessons
> yet again.
>
> But please
> don't turn the light switch yet
> as valuable and friendly
> as the darkness is
> leave the porch light on
> for contrast.

Pictures in the hallway,
paintings up above the stairs
clippings we collect
and only look at once.

So much is saved
held in escrow
kept as security
for times to come
or to remind us
of the times
we know will never
        come again.

Life should have a game plan
        but it doesn't.
Need should know
exactly where it's going,
but it seldom does.

The photographs didn't arrive right away. In their stead came more information on Rodney Marion McKune. The initial discovery of McKune was disclosed in an entry in the *1923 Los Angeles City Directory*, which stated that a Rodney M. McKune described as "a lumberman" lived at 1218 South Indiana Street. The name did not appear before or after 1923. In 1923 a Hugh McKone was listed at 1204 South Indiana. On January 19, 1976, Hugh McKone's widow, Mrs. Helena McKone, was interviewed and recalled living on South Indiana in 1923. She did not recognize the name Rodney McKune. A search was made of the following records in Los Angeles County:

Births:	1895 to 1933
Deaths:	1920 to 1933
Marriages:	1900 to 1933
Recorders' indexes:	1915 to 1928
Divorce records:	1921 to 1930

This search provided the following documents: a certificate of marriage for Rodney M. McKune in Los Angeles and a divorce action.

On November 12, 1921, Rodney M. McKune was married. The groom was described as single, this being his first marriage; born in Colorado, twenty-five years old, employed in the lumber business and living in Los Angeles. His father was listed as Julien D. McKune, born in Pennsylvania; and his mother, Martha Mallette, born in Kansas. The bride was described as widowed; this would be her second marriage. She was twenty-five years old, and living in Los Angeles. There was a witness to the ceremony, an A. G. Rivera, also of Los

Angeles, and the wedding was performed by Justice of the Peace Edward Judson Brown.

Later investigation would show that the groom was born in 1900, so was twenty-one rather than twenty-five in November, 1921. Apparently in those days Madison Avenue's brainwashing had already begun and it was perhaps considered proper for the groom to be older, or at least the same age, as his bride.

Rodney Marion McKune was born on February 6, 1900, in Blue Creek Park, Colorado, and his military service record described him as single despite the fact that he was married at the time he enlisted in the Army at Fort Mac-Arthur, California, on December 12, 1923. At that time he was 5' 9½", weighed 144 pounds, and had 20-20 vision in both eyes. Having discovered much of his military service record in the divorce action instituted by his wife, Green's agency instructed investigators in Denver, Colorado, to search for his birth certificate. The search took six days and provided the following: thirteen different places in 1900 with the name Blue Creek, Blue Park, Blue River, etc. "We found a Blue Creek in Blue Park in Saguache County, Colorado. In checking records in these places, voting registrations, etc., we failed to find anyone by the name Rodney Marion McKune or McKuien, or anyone by the name of McKuen at that period of time."

The search continued at the Federal Center in Denver where all the census records are on file. After reviewing the microfilms, the investigators again drew a blank. Still in Denver, the birth and death records failed to turn up anyone with the subject's name. The various McKunes (whatever their spellings) living in the Denver area were contacted by telephone. The majority had no relatives by that name or knowledge of anyone named Rodney M. McKune. More checks. The counties of Arapahoe, Adams, Clear Creek, and Gilpin: nothing on the subject or his relatives was turned up. Numerous long distance calls were made to various cities in Colorado but the results all came back negative.

At the end the Denver investigators concluded that there may have been some error in the name of the town where he was born. It could be another town of similar spelling.

I was reading the report now with considerable detachment. Having set out on this latest phase of my quest months ago, feeling somehow sure my father would finally be found, I'd begun lately to think that perhaps it was enough that along the way I'd learned a great many new things about my mother, my other relatives—and about myself.

But there was more to come on the man from Blue Creek or Blue Park or wherever.

Apparently the McKune marriage was in trouble before Rodney's enlistment, for in the divorce action his wife listed desertion as the main cause. She claimed he had deserted her beginning the day he enlisted. This, despite a photocopy of a letter from Rodney full of endearments and promising that he was trying to get a furlough and a little extra money to buy her a present. He was stationed in Oklahoma then and presumably that's where the divorce action reached him. He did not contest the divorce, and an interlocutory judgment by default was filed November 26, 1926. Final divorce papers were filed on November 30 of the same year.

Beyond the personal endearments and the gripes about Army inspections, I found McKune's letter to his wife fascinating. To begin with, his handwriting was very much like my own, a little more legible perhaps, but not much. He spoke of the Mitchell case: "I noticed in today's paper where the court had found him guilty. Believe me, he sure has said a lot of truths. I had big hopes of his winning, for the Air Service would be much different then." Presumably he was speaking of the trial of Billy Mitchell. He seems to have had some perception of the future. His letter went on to say they were having some very pretty weather for December and that there was some kind of excitement in Lawton because "they have brought in some wells near here now and that being the case, things should start to boom around here." The letter concluded, "Well, little one, you remember I told you that you had rather a good hold on me and it is just the same now as it has always been in the past. There is no woman but you that interests me in any way. It is my little [here the word becomes illegible but is obviously an endearment] and I still meet you in my dreams, so you see it is impossible for me to forget my nice 'Little Dream Lady,' for just as I close my eyes at night, you are always last on my mind. Well, sweetheart, I will say bye-bye for this time. So with all my love and kisses, I am as ever, your old Rodney."

Near his signature he drew a flower. I won't speculate on how many thousands of people can attest to the fact that more often than not, in signing an autograph I scrawl a flower beside it.

Rodney Marion McKune was discharged from the Army in December, 1926. He did go to work in the oil fields in Oklahoma. In 1928 or 1929 he was injured on an oil rig in Texas. He called his sister Laura in Utah and she arranged with her stepfather, Julien McKune, who owned the McKune sawmill, to send money to his son so he could return to Utah. Once home, he went to work for his father as foreman.

The Utah mill was a modest family operation, situated in the hills above Altonah. Until his father's death in 1939 or 1940, he worked at his job steadily. After his father's death he took charge. His mother had died about 1937.

In 1930 Rodney married Maude McNabb, the mill's cook. Maude had been married twice before and was twenty years his senior. Despite the misgivings of Mrs. McNabb's three sons by her first two marriages, the union seemed to work out.

In 1943 the mill was sold to cover bad debts and the

couple went to visit Maude's sister Phon at her home in Kansas. Soon after, they came to live in Davis, California. That was roughly in 1946. (As a passing reference, Maude's first husband was named McElhenny. He had been murdered, leaving her a widow. She then married a man named McNabb, who subsequently deserted her. The "Mc's" of this world, it would seem, are endless.) For nearly twenty years afterward Rodney McKune worked at the Union Ice Company in Santa Monica, California. His Social Security number was 524-30-7963.

Having checked all the Blue Creeks, Blue Parks, and Blue Rivers in Colorado and finding no birth certificate for McKune, it turns out that he was born in Mexico while his mother and father were working there. This information nearly completed the man's dossier.

His history, painstakingly put together, would seem to rule him out as my father, particularly because there was no way of placing him in Oakland, California, or anywhere in the San Francisco Bay Area during 1932. And so it looked as though yet another lead had petered out.

I have learned no new alphabet this week.
No new yardstick different from the last time out.
The old language has had to do too long a time.
I use the past arithmetic
       to make the present work.
Yet even going from room to room
I walk with arms outstreched.

While the investigators were busy tracing and tracking down more leads, my own investigation intensified. I started opening my mail with more care, and no matter how remote a possibility seemed I tried my best not to discount it.

Many of the leads I myself followed could be taken care of with merely a letter asking key questions. I spent hours on the phone tracking down people in at least twenty states. And I was up and down the coast of California by airplane or car dozens of times meeting people and checking out stories until I began to feel that I might well qualify for a job as a private investigator, though secretly I knew that I would have to go a long way to be in the same league with the firm already assigned the job.

On February 1 I went to a Montana rest home to meet a woman named Christiansen, who had informed me in a long and very lucid letter that her original married name had been McKuen. She even thought it possible her ex-husband, now living in the Midwest, might indeed be my father.

The rest home, which I shall call Easyrest, was a depressing, dark, foreboding house set on an acre of weeds and dead trees. It looked as though it belonged more properly in a Gothic novel. Squinting, one could almost see the girl in the purple dress on the edge of the cliff and the old house in the background with its shutters banging. There was, however, nothing romantic about this building and the inhabitants—some two dozen senior citizens, age sixty and up, who lived, or rather existed, amid some of the worst squalor I'd ever seen. The rest home was privately owned, and in talking to Mrs. Christiansen I learned that most of the people were there because relatives had paid handsomely to keep them out of the way. Though some had been shunted aside and shut away for as many as ten and fifteen years, presumably outliving their relatives' expectations, most seemed to have an attitude not so much of resignation but of determination. Each appeared resolved to live with as much dignity as possible under such pitiful circumstances. If their relatives didn't want them, then they didn't want to be with their relatives. Most had had no visitors since their arrival.

Mrs. Christiansen was a pleasant lady whose daughter and son-in-law had paid for her internment at Easyrest. While I find it hard to understand why anyone would want to dispose of someone close to them merely because they had reached a certain age, or because they had become inconvenient or didn't fit in, I was really puzzled at such an intelligent and valuable human being as this lady being put out to any pasture, let alone this ugly, unpleasant place. I saw her for about three hours a day for four days. With her help I was able to locate her ex-husband, now living in North Dakota and remarried. I pieced together his movements during the late twenties and early thirties. He was not the man I was looking for. I think I knew that after my first talk with Mrs. Christiansen, but because I enjoyed talking with her so much I came back to continue the conversation.

Meanwhile in northern California, Joy Orr was shown a series of photographs to see if she could identify any of the young men pictured as the "Mack" she had known in the Stanford Hotel in Oakland in the early thirties. None faintly reminded her of the man who had lived with Clarice Woolever.

The photographs of Rodney Marion McKune were then specifically pointed out to Mrs. Orr. The answer was still no; in her judgment "Mack" and Rodney Marion McKune were not the same person.

She was then asked if she was able to determine with more certainty the date she first met Clarice. No, but she still believed it was as early as 1930. This isn't possible since my mother didn't move to the East Bay until the last of April, 1931. She appears in the San Francisco telephone directory as late as June, 1930. And since the listings would have to be submitted several months prior to the date of the directory edition, it's unlikely that she had moved to Oakland prior to late spring of 1931.

On January 26 Dewey and Gladys Younger had been interviewed at their residence in northern California. Rodney

Marion McKune was Mrs. Younger's uncle by marriage. Mrs. Younger's maiden name is Kilgore. Her Aunt Maude had married McKune in Altonah, Utah, on July 11, 1930. Everyone in the family thought it was an unusual marriage because of the age difference. Maude had worked for McKune's father at first as a cook and then a bookkeeper. It was while Rodney was the foreman that he and Maude met, fell in love, and were married.

At that time Gladys and Dewey Younger were living in Hawaii. They had been married in November, 1929, and lived in Hawaii until the war broke out in 1941. Afterward they moved to Texas where they lived for five years, and finally settled down in California in 1946. So Gladys Younger's knowledge of Maude's marriage to Rodney McKune was all secondhand and came mostly from letters she received from her mother, who was then living in Wyoming.

Gladys knew Maude had had some reservations about marrying a man twenty years her junior. Maude had sought the approval of other members of her family, "My brother had considered the marriage a mistake, she wanted his blessing but he didn't even know the man. I think he eventually told her she should do what she wanted to do."

The Youngers themselves didn't meet Rodney until after World War II when both families were living in California. They were quite certain that Rodney and Maude had continued to live in Utah until after the beginning of the war and that during those years Rodney had continued to work at the mill and Maude still did the cooking and bookkeeping. Of course they hadn't been anywhere near the couple, so they couldn't be absolutely sure.

Asked if Rodney had ever been a salesman, either of refrigerators or musical instruments, the Youngers replied they had never heard that to be the case—"All he ever knew was lumber and ice." They had no idea if Rodney liked to dance or if he had any musical talents. Asked whether Rodney McKune had been in the San Francisco Bay Area in 1932, they said they didn't know. But both Dewey and Gladys felt strongly that it was improbable.

"He was a foreman at his father's lumber company. He never left—or we never heard about it—he couldn't leave the mill—it was way up in the mountains and they had to come down to the town to buy food. I don't think they were away from each other for one night. In the 1920s I might agree, but not in the 1930s.

"Right before Maude died in 1960 Rodney told me if he had it to do all over again, he would.

"I don't believe they had the money for him to be making trips. They were happy. She was a little bit afraid of the difference in their ages, but she seemed to think he was all right otherwise. I first met him in 1946—they'd been married for sixteen years by that time—I'd heard no complaints, but I can't verify it."

The Youngers were convinced that at no time had they ever had any indication that the marriage between Rodney and Maude had been an unhappy one, and that had there been any serious marital difficulties between them they would have inevitably have heard about it sooner or later. From the tone of Gladys and Dewey Younger's interview, which went on at a much longer length than the few paragraphs I've quoted here, I considered them to be very honest and helpful people.

Still, in reading the report, it is impossible to ignore the fact that for the first sixteen years of Rodney and Maude's marriage the Youngers were living what might well have been a half a world away. Despite the current interest in therapy and true confession, families didn't always broadcast their marital problems, particularly to relatives who had so obviously opposed the union in the first place. The Youngers knew so little of Rodney's background that they were totally unaware he had been previously married.

At one point Dewey referred to Rodney McKune as the black sheep of his family. I loved the thought of my father being the black sheep of the family as much as I enjoyed the idea of being conceived in a hotel room. If this man were indeed a sheep who strayed, perhaps we had much in common.

When asked if they knew anything about Rodney's activities before the marriage in 1930, the Youngers said they believed he'd spent some time in California during the 1920s. They thought that was one of the reasons why Rodney had decided to settle in California after leaving Utah.

"He used to talk about San Francisco, but I think he was a single man then," Mrs. Younger volunteered. "That was back in the days when he was in the service. We don't know much about that. He was a roamer—but he didn't roam after he was married. That was all before the marriage. Maude knew all about him after that."

Was it possible that Rodney McKune had come to California in 1932 to seek a new job with the idea of sending for his wife after he was finally settled? It *was* the Depression, and small family businesses everywhere were falling apart. Theirs was not the only mill that was to shut down before the oncoming war's end.

The Youngers were shown the sketch made from Mrs. Orr's description of the "Mack" whom she met at the Stanford Hotel. Both said it didn't resemble Rodney McKune. The Youngers both said it was their personal opinion that Rodney Marion McKune was not the man any of us were searching for. "It's just not possible—he didn't have the funds to be traveling around—he had to operate that mill and that was it," they said.

Just as Mrs. Orr was unable to identify the photographs supplied by the Youngers, they in turn were now unable to identify the man in the sketch.

But Depression or not, it takes very little money to travel around the country. A steady thumb and patience can get you almost anywhere, even now. Despite local or national figures concerning unemployment, any able-bodied man can get a job if he wants one. Temporary or otherwise. It would have taken very little talent on the part of McKune to obtain an interim job as a salesman. After all, he had worked as one before and would again.

Could he have gone to the Bay Area in 1932 on mill business? Overstayed his time and met my mother?

Isn't it possible that a quarrel followed by a separation occurred and maybe a month or two, or even a year or two later, the couple got back together? Why did every move have to be substantiated by a railway ticket or a fact? Nobody was on trial; there was no jury to convince and no verdict to be brought in. Of course, I knew the answer to these questions. I, too, wanted to know for sure that the man we hoped eventually to find was beyond any doubt the right one.

Phon Wilson, a sister of the late Maude McKune, is eighty-five and living in Kansas. The investigator sensed she was maintaining a protective attitude about Maude and her family. Though Mrs. Wilson has lived in Kansas most of her life, she said she had kept in close communication with Maude by letter. She felt confident she would have been aware of any serious difficulties in her sister's marriage. Nothing in any letter had led her to believe that Maude and Rodney had ever had any real problems. As she described it, the marriage had been "very congenial."

Really? If she had been among those opposing the marriage in the first place, would her sister be likely to confide in her over a marital spat?

Phon Wilson didn't meet Rodney McKune until the early 1940s. She did know that Rodney had been married once before but didn't think he had any family of his own to speak of. She confirmed that Maude had three sons by her first two marriages. The youngest, Danny McNabb, is deceased. Rodney apparently looked upon him as his own son.

Calls were placed to various lumber companies in Salt Lake City, Utah, to get the names of some old-timers in the business.

Clarence Jones painted a rosy picture of Rodney and Maude. He said that they had "lived it up like a couple of kids." He didn't recall Rodney making any trips at all during the early thirties and remembered that they lived in a cabin at the mill and stuck pretty close together. Jones had worked for the mill even before Rodney married Maude McNabb and was there until the McKune mill had been liquidated for debts in 1943.

He knew that they had left for California after the sawmill was sold, but was almost positive that neither of them ever left the area before except for small vacation trips of about a week's duration. "They always went together."

Jones added that "While all the mills were hard hit by the Depression, the McKunes' sawmill made a good living, although it didn't make much money during that period." He confirmed the foreclosure and sale in 1943.

Scanning the report, I'm amazed at the accuracy, even more than the inaccuracy, of people's memories of forty-two years ago. Particularly since I have a very poor memory myself for time and individual circumstances. It's been hard, therefore, for me to be completely convinced that Rodney Marion McKune might not have taken that trip to California during the thirties.

Laura Preece, also living in Utah, is Rodney Marion McKune's sister. She has lived in the Vernal area since the time before her brother went into the Army. Although in her eighties, she is as bright and clearheaded as a thirty-year-old and very interested in my search. Mrs. Preece said Rodney first went to Southern California in about 1919. He married his cousin in 1921 and then joined the Army—she said that Rodney was divorced sometime in the 1920s and that Rodney went to Texas and worked in the oil fields for a few years. As far as Mrs. Preece knows, Rodney never left Utah from the time he married Maude in 1930 until he sold the mill in 1943.

She doesn't recall Rodney or Maude ever separating or taking any business trips. She remembers that Rodney's first job after arriving in Santa Monica was as a "fire watch" in the parks and forests above that city. After about two years, he went to work for the Union Ice Company in Los Angeles. Mrs. Preece said Rodney had loved California and always wanted to go back there. According to her, Rodney sold the mill because he tired of the hard work and of getting snowed-in every year up in the hills.

Mrs. Preece finished the conversation by saying she'd sure enjoy having me as a nephew although she didn't think it was the case. "At any rate," she added, "tell him to come and visit me anytime he likes." I immediately checked my schedule, canceled a concert, and called the airlines.

Mrs. Edith Lang is Rodney's other sister. As far as her knowledge goes, Rodney never even left Utah after marrying in 1930—that is, not until he moved to California in 1943. She doesn't even recall a vacation trip, unless it was to Provo or Salt Lake City. If they did go, they went together and as far as Mrs. Lang knows they never went outside the state. She is sure that it was in an Oklahoma (not Texas) oil field that her brother was injured in about 1929.

Walter M. Wiskie worked for the Union Ice Company for about forty-two years. The name Rodney Marion McKune means nothing to him, but he did not start in Oakland until 1936. Informed that McKune may have been a salesman, he suggested contacting Clinton Milman in Berkeley. Wiskie said Milman is the only salesman from those days who still is alive, and there's a sharp distinction between being a salesman and an iceman in the Union Ice organization. According to Wiskie, the Union Ice Company employees formerly belonged to the Ice Wagon Drivers Union, which merged with the Frozen Drivers Union. Clinton Milman died a year ago. The name Rodney Marion McKune meant nothing to his widow.

Sofas became davenports. Victrolas became phonographs and finally stereo equipment. Although a milkman is still a milkman, it's very possible that an iceman might, even in the days when refrigerators (still called iceboxes today by some) were not so plentiful, decide it was preferable to term himself a refrigerator salesman rather than an iceman. Perhaps the woman he was seeing would even do that for him.

I cannot look back
       far enough,
nor can I go beyond
the grove of trees
that sit like rows
       of ghosts
fencing me off
from whatever past
I may or may not have.

He might be
just beyond those trees
or beyond another dozen
rows of unmarked pine,
but where,
       which tree?

Come forward, damn you
and be recognized
        and heard.
Stretch out your hand
        to me
and mine will come back
to you in return.

I only want
to see your eyes
and prove that they
        match mine.

I don't want from you
        your name
I'm satisfied I have it.
I'll make no claim
on your insurance.
Tell your newer heirs
        they can relax.

I'll be satisfied
to touch you once
so that I can
        put an end
to my beginning.

On Friday, the thirteenth of February, 1976, the photographs of Rodney Marion McKune arrived. One showed
him in riding breeches with boots laced nearly to his knees. It
was taken in 1930. The second, taken fourteen years later,
pictured him in what might have been a uniform of some
sort, maybe even an iceman's uniform. On the other hand,
they could have been merely matching shirt and trousers. It
was unbelievable. In comparing photographs taken of me at
the same ages, there is no doubt that the man is my father.

Rodney Marion and Maude McKune,
at the mill, Utah.

Rodney and Maude
in Santa Monica, 1948

Rod McKuen

On November 4, 1963, Rodney Marion McKune died in Los Angeles County. He died of occlusive calcitic coronary arteriosclerosis in the UCLA Medical Center and was buried on November 8, 1963, in the Woodlawn Cemetery. At the time he was living at 1637 Franklin Street, Santa Monica. I was living less than twenty miles away at 1302 North Gardner Street in Los Angeles.

How do I know that Rodney Marion McKune is my father? I know, that's all. For me, looking at those photographs taken so long ago was like looking into a mirror.

Then there's the name. I can't believe any mother would name her son Rodney Marvin if a Rodney Marion hadn't preceded him. That doesn't mean the stories given out by the people who allegedly knew my mother, particularly the women, were untrue. They have consistency to them. Some of the dates are slightly incorrect, some of the addresses are mixed up or at variance, but those women knew enough about my mother to have known her.

Whether she was a taxi dancer before or after my birth is of little importance to me. Whether she lived at one hotel or another doesn't matter much. For instance, I'm convinced the man she was going with when Joy Orr knew her was another man. (I assume in those days young girls were allowed more than one boyfriend as they grew up.) I believe that "Mac" McKuien and Rodney Marion McKune are the same person. I don't think he and my mother had a very long relationship. On the other hand, if my father and his wife in Utah were having a difficult period in their marriage, his relationship with Mom might have lasted as long as six months.

Who knows how long my father's visit was to California? Everybody who knew him talked about how much he liked the state, and he did eventually come here and settle down. It is a pity that I never knew him, because I think I would have liked him. I believe my mother either knew about his marriage and wanted to throw people off the track with the "Mac" story or loved him a great deal and was afraid that if he knew about her pregnancy he might feel the necessity of divorcing to marry her rather than expressing any real love. My mother was a very proud woman and she wouldn't have wanted that.

Relatives of Rodney Marion McKune living in Kansas and Texas are sure he was never in the San Francisco–Oakland Bay area in 1932. However, none of them saw the man during that year or for several years after. None have letters written to them from my father, who allegedly lived in Utah all that time. It is doubtful that a wife they disapproved of would have written and told them anything regarding marital troubles the two might be having. Forty-four years ago is a long time, and the remaining relatives on my father's side are basing their statements on a *feel* rather than any bona fide evidence.

If my newfound aunts can assume, why can't I? It is quite possible that Rodney Marion McKune, who incurred a bad leg injury while working in the oil fields, might have gone to San Francisco as late as 1932 to see a specialist. Old injuries do act up. Old injuries can provide excuses for "getting away."

In addition to saying he was single when he entered the

Army, he took four years off his age in obtaining a marriage license to marry his first wife in 1923. This is confirmed by the birth, marriage, and death certificates. Isn't it possible he might have lied to my mother about his age? That would account for the 27 (?) given as my father's age on my birth certificate.

The coincidence of Rodney Marion and Rodney Marvin cannot be explained away. Even if it could, a man who took every opportunity to talk about California and visit it and finally settled down in the state outside of Davis, as a forest ranger, and afterward for the rest of his life worked as an iceman in Santa Monica, doesn't build on the conjecture; it only adds to the coincidence.

I knew, of course, that he was my father the moment I saw the first photographs. His handwriting is uncannily like mine. Like me, he spent much of his early life as a loner—running away, traveling, and taking up a number of loner occupations. According to relatives, among other jobs we shared were that of salesman, forest ranger, farmer, and mechanic. (Apparently he was as bad a mechanic as I am and once took an automobile apart and was unable to put it together again.) I even worked in the oil fields in Oklahoma and Texas for a short spell.

In our twenties and in our forties we were roughly the same weight and build, had the same color eyes and hair, and even the same blood type. While this is not conclusive evidence itself to the outsider—or even to the man searching for his identity—compound it with the fact that photographs of both of his wives looked a good deal like my mother in her later years. Some men are repeatedly drawn to look-alike women.

Isn't it odd that while forty years ago the Mormon Church was widely recognized, it had nowhere near the membership it has today? Yet, two of my mother's best friends, Hilda and Jean Nielsen, were Mormons coming out of Union, Oregon, hardly a predominantly Mormon town. Rodney Marion McKune was from the seat of the Mormon Church, Utah, and my mother actually managed to find a man in Nevada—the only Mormon in his family—who was to become my stepfather. My mother and her family had been Catholic, yet when I turned eight, it was she more than my stepfather who insisted that I be baptized Mormon—incidentally, the first of six baptisms I've had so far in my lifetime (I keep changing churches through inquisitiveness and the need to grow).

I called and wrote letters to the church. Finally I found a man, Lawrence Ranger, who had worked with the church records during the 1930s, and according to him my father paid no tithings to the church during 1932. "This was not uncommon," said Ranger, who now lives near Provo, Utah, "because the Depression brought about mass unemployment and therefore a lack of revenue. I didn't pay a tithing either, but then I was away and broke. Still, then as now, no Mormon ever went on relief, which is one of the many points of the tithing."

He didn't remember Maude McKune or Rodney applying for any assistance from the church, nor were there any records attesting to that fact. Without my even framing the next question, Ranger announced quietly, "I don't believe Rodney was baptized a Mormon."

I redialed my newfound Aunt in Utah.

"No," she answered, "Rodney was never a Mormon but I am."

"Thanks," I replied, somewhat weakly. "Oh, and I'm coming to see you Wednesday."

"Good! Maybe you *are* my nephew. I hope so."

I redialed Ranger. "How well did you know McKune?"

"We were pals," he answered, "real pals."

"In thirty-one—no, I think it was the summer of 1932—we drove out to California together."

I think my heart stopped.

My God, here was a man able to put my father in the right place at the right time just as the other witnesses—not witnesses at all because they were not in close proximity to my father at that period—were sure that he was more than likely not in California. There was no way for Ranger to know how important it was for me to establish Rodney Marion McKune as being in the San Francisco–Oakland Bay area during August of 1932 when I was conceived. But he had.

Here was the scale: On one side my father's relatives saying they didn't think he was in California at that time, but *not one* who could present absolute evidence. A father who had a chronic need to run away, who always talked about California and dreamed of settling there; a wife twenty years his senior who during that period did not get along with relatives, either hers or his, because relatives on both sides disapproved of the marriage. People in their eighties and nineties being asked to stretch their memories back to something as unimportant as what someone else was doing forty-odd years ago.

The balance shifts drastically when you combine photographs of Rodney Marion and Rodney Marvin. Forget that they had the same blood type, same build and coloring and, in later years, the same deep furrows on either side of their noses; ignore the traits they had in common—running away, drifting, holding down a variety of jobs and moving on when they felt like it, a love of California, and the loner syndrome.

The facts: Rodney Marion McKune chose wives or women who were look-alikes of his first wife: he and a friend drove to California the summer I was conceived. There was positive proof of that just as there was no real proof, only hearsay from people not in any real position to know where he was, who didn't even adamantly insist that he remained in Utah.

Where was he in 1932? Well, among other places in Oakland, California, for a short spell, dancing at the Rose Room where he met an attractive young woman with whom he helped conceive a child, and for some reason—probably that he was married and this was only a passing affair to him, or quite possibly because he never knew he was to become a father—he went away.

However my father felt, whether he knew or didn't know about me, one thing was obvious. Even though she decided to bring me up by herself, my mother loved the man enough to give me his name—probably, if nothing more, to remind herself and make indelible the memory of whatever time they spent together. Change one letter in my second name and Rodney Marvin becomes Rodney Marion. As for the last name, we already know that there are more than seventy-five ways to spell it. My mother had her version; two birth certificates had yet other versions and for all I know, I might have been the one who long ago invented the spelling I now use. Here again, you have merely to invert one letter in the last name to come up with the same spelling.

My father died only eight years earlier than my mother. Both died too young and should be living today. So far as I know, there is no one alive who could make the evidence for either side stronger. I'm still tying up loose ends, and even if I can't put everyone else's mind to rest, I'm certainly able to satisfy my own thoughts as to who my father was.

Green concurs and thinks that there is little doubt that Rodney Marion McKune and "Mack" McKuien are one and the same.

I'm a lot richer today than I ever deserved to be or dreamed of being. I've been made wealthy by all those people who came forward to help me find my father. So many people that I don't even know, who offered help and kindness during the seemingly impossible search that has taken me three-quarters of my lifetime. Obviously I owe debts to people I will never be able to pay—for kindness, thoughtfulness, and just plain caring—not to mention the hours of honest work by those who can't possibly know how important it was for me to learn a little more about my roots. In the process I found out a great deal more about myself and my mother.

I've said before that I haven't minded living my life, but I sure as hell wouldn't want to go back and relive it. Of course I've been doing just that on a crash basis over the past six months. Looking at it, assessing it again, I hope the results when finally tabulated will have made me a better, more compassionate man for having looked for and found my father.

During this recent investigation I had a chance to do a lot of talking as well as thinking. I stated in at least one radio interview that I had been able to reduce nearly all things around me to threes, and somehow I had always had the strong belief in the *three syndrome* whether one was speaking of morning, afternoon, or evening; the Blessed Trinity; birth, life, and death; or any true art which in order to have permanent impact must have a beginning, a middle, and an end. A novel, short story, painting, play, piece of sculpture—or a song. Art to be art has a premise, a destination, and in between a vehicle for traveling there. Art transports, but the vehicle is not the art form. Life is given us to carry along, but the shell we keep it in isn't necessarily the best part of us we show the world.

A friend of mine, Dr. Darwin Shannon, a nuclear physicist who lectures and teaches at UCLA, heard an interview I gave where I discussed my theory of threes. He told me I was not alone in my analogy and, whether I knew it or not, a scientist named Jell-Mann at Cal Tech had developed the same theory concerning particles of matter. Until his theory it was assumed that a neutron or a proton or the heavier particles (hadrons) existed of themselves. Jell-Mann has now been able to break matter down into three separate parts so that each heavy particle is composed of three distinct quarks. The matter is matter only when the three parts are collected together. I believe life itself comes in three stages—a further breakdown than birth, life, and death (each of which could be broken down to three additional parts).

I have lately perceived my life as entering the third stage—the one I consider to be the most productive and the one in which I will finally find out what it is I was meant to do here in this place. The two previous periods in my life have such obvious distinctions from each other, that this third one is only a logical extension of the first two. Or rather it is totally different but could not have started or hoped to succeed without the previous periods that have gone before it.

Friends have seen and I have seen within myself so many changes in and around me that I don't feel I'm the same as I was last year. I don't believe that basically this has anything to do with normal growth, getting older, realigning my values, taking stock of myself, or any of the things one attributes change to. It is merely that I am entering and have entered the third and final phase of my life. I am so conscious of it and so aware of when it started happening that I could almost point with certainty to the exact moment I awoke to discover one door closing as another opened up.

That I would seek out and find my father at the beginning of this third part of my life has helped me to overcome one of the final hurdles that would have slowed the beginning of that phase. The quest for specific knowledge has caused me to stumble on knowledge of a different kind.

24

A string untied
needs tying up
as every empty space
to merely prove
its own existence
needs walking through.

While mystery is a mainstay
the lack of knowledge
on a chosen subject
needs the miner's pick,
the mason's trowel
and the astronomer's
strict surveyor's gaze.

Dinosaurs
once walked the earth

but where?
I haven't been there.

How many comets
 have I charted
as they arched across
the winter sky then fell?
None has fallen
near enough for me to see
the well it dug on impact.
If I traveled
every hour of every day
through the second half
of my own lifetime
there would still be spaces
I'd have liked to fill
if only for an hour.

Some things demand
a finding out
as some loose strings
 need tying
and so a map is brought out
xed and circled and gone over.

The airport at Vernal, Utah, is little more than a couple of runways with a low, shedlike structure of about three rooms housing a bomb inspection unit, car rental, ticket counter, baggage claim, and waiting room. I was in a hurry to meet my aunt and it seemed as though the ground crew had no intention of removing the baggage from the aircraft that had just brought me there.

It was a hot Wednesday afternoon in the middle of May, 1976, too hot to stay inside the building, so I moved outside and stood for a long time leaning against the fence, watching the passengers go along the field and up the steps into the plane for the continuation of its journey. Apparently the new passengers had to be loaded before our baggage was unloaded. I struck up a conversation with a husky blond man in his thirties who was also waiting for his luggage to arrive.

"Do you think we'll ever get it?"

"I don't know, maybe the only way is to check back in on the aircraft and continue flying. But this time I'll take a parachute. Say, aren't you—"

I cut him off by asking for directions to the little town my aunt was living in.

"I dunno," he said, "I don't come here very often."

It turned out he was from Dinosaur, Colorado, and worked not far from there mining magonite. We had begun talking without introducing ourselves and I still hadn't determined what he was doing in Vernal. He seemed equally puzzled as to why I was there.

"There's the baggage," he said.

I looked up in time to see the pilot and copilot of the plane I'd just arrived on unloading the baggage. The car I'd rented had arrived and I determined there and then that rather than take this flight back, I'd drive from Vernal to Salt Lake City after the meeting with my aunt. I could stay overnight in Salt Lake and fly out to Los Angeles in the morning.

As I was closing the trunk, the man from Dinosaur brushed past me and said, "Naw, you couldn't be—I mean, not in *Vernal, Utah.*"

I stopped in town, bought some records for my aunt— in the rush I'd forgotten to bring any along. Wayne Massie, who works at Stanyan in Los Angeles between photojournalism assignments, had accompanied me in order to photograph me with my newfound aunt. The directions were easy to follow and we pulled up in front of Laura Preece's house less than two hours after leaving the Vernal airport.

As she greeted me at the screen door, almost the first

words out of Mrs. Preece's mouth were: "You can call me Aunt Laura." I was immensely pleased, because her sister had been almost positive there was no possibility of a mysterious *nephew* turning up. But Laura, having seen me on television shortly after the first interview she gave to the detective agency, was convinced there was a strong possibility of my being her brother's son.

I spent a marvelous afternoon with her, looking over old pictures that she had carefully organized. Many were of Rodney and Maude, and many more of his adopted son by Maude's first marriage, Danny McNabb, who had killed himself while still a young man. Yet another tragedy in Maude's life. There were photographs of the mill, truckloads of logs being brought to it and lumber being taken away.

Laura's grandson, Bill Preece, now a grown man and a banker with his own family, living and working in Salt Lake City, had come down for the day to visit his grandmother. I asked him if the mill still existed. "The last time I went up there, there were just some piles of sawdust," he replied.

"I'd like to offer you some coffee," Mrs. Preece apologized, "but we're Mormons and don't drink coffee. I wasn't always a Mormon but I like being with the church now. . . . You know, you really do look like Rodney. I can't say for sure you're his son, but I sure believe you are."

I was shown photos of my grandfather. It was uncanny. In some of the pictures I looked more like him than I did my father. I told her how amazed I was that so many people were convinced I couldn't possibly be this man's son and yet none of them had any way of proving it. Some didn't know; others hadn't seen Rodney for several years before I was conceived and many years after.

"It doesn't matter to me whether you're my nephew or not," Laura said. "As far as I'm concerned, I'll adopt you." I told her it was the best offer I'd had in recent memory and she seemed pleased.

Laura Preece lives in a modest white house with a screened porch. Inside, the living room is comfortable and contains a rocking chair, a huge overstuffed sofa and chair, and photos of her grandchildren and great-grandchildren are proudly and prominently displayed everywhere. She complained that the davenport needed to be re-covered, but she hated to do so since the cat would just continue to scratch away at it. The furniture looked fine to me. The kitchen is practical and obviously used. One bedroom contains an old high bed that she must have had for many years.

Laura Preece's husband had been a handsome man, and she has many photographs of him and talked about him often, but only as part of the general conversation. Draped over the couch we sat on as we talked was a multicolored Indian blanket that must have been woven more than a hundred years ago. The house seemed full of beautiful and personal things but not overcrowded in the least or cluttered the way Mama, who was as big a pack rat as I am, made the places we lived in.

She brought out two wooden horseheads that had been crudely carved by my father to make stick horses for Laura's children. On a bookcase there was another wooden horsehead my father must have made. A little more care and time seemed to have gone into this sculpture.

My aunt seemed proud of her equestrian abilities as a young woman and there were several photographs of her astride different mounts. Her graduation picture showed her to be one of the prettiest girls I've seen, in or out of a photograph.

We looked at more pictures. Wayne took photographs of the two of us together, and finally, reluctantly, I said my good-byes. By then Bill Preece's wife had arrived with their three children (Laura's great-grandchildren). I shook hands all around, said good-bye to my aunt, and was halfway down the front yard to the car when she called me back.

Rod and Laura, 1976.

Julien D. McKune.

The McKune sawmill.

Rodney and friends at the mill, early 30s.

Rodney Marion, 1930s.

"Yes, I think you are Rodney's son," she confided. "I can't be sure because I wasn't there. My grandson and his wife both think so too. Don't let anyone tell you Rodney isn't your father."

"I hope you'll come and see me in California," I said.

"I'd love to; my son lives in Las Vegas and I usually get out there to see him twice a year. He's been trying to get me to move to Las Vegas because of what happened two years ago. I was attacked by an Indian who came right up to the door. That's why I still limp. Bill says I can stay here two more years or one more Indian, but I hate to leave, you know. This is my home."

In the photographs I'd seen earlier there were many of Laura with her Ute Indian friends. She'd grown up with all kinds of people and seemed to be devoid of all prejudice. Saying she was attacked by an Indian was the same as saying she was attacked by Fred, if she'd known his name, or a man in a blue suit wearing black patent-leather gloves and an eye-patch, had she had that good a description of her assailant.

"I can't imagine why anyone would want to attack a nice lady like you," I commented, trying not to be patronizing since I didn't feel that way at all.

"There are some crazy people who do crazy things," she said.

Again we said good-bye. "I'm your Aunt Laura," she reminded me, "and remember, don't let anyone tell you Rodney isn't your dad."

The drive to Salt Lake City was uneventful: a cup of coffee along the way at a truck stop whose name and location I have no intention of remembering. Most of all, I had two hours and more to think about the lady I'd just met who was now and would always be part of my family. I liked her so much that I genuinely envied her grandson, who'd had the benefit of so many years with this upbeat, gentle, hardworking, and friendly lady. I was happy about finding and meeting her, yes, but let down because I was getting older and so was she; though probably I sensed it more than she did, since I think she has no intention of getting old—and I would like to spend twenty or thirty years getting to know my Aunt Laura.

Wayne suggested we go out and have a beer. "It'll cheer you up," he said. "Besides, it's a full moon; you never can tell what'll happen."

Out we went. If you've never been to Salt Lake City and don't realize there are two separate streets, North Temple and South Temple, not to mention East Temple and West Temple, and that the same holds true for nearly every street in the downtown area. There's no way you could possibly have a conception of how long it took us to find the friendly neighborhood bar, about five blocks away.

It was like any other bar. The people were pleasant and I had more than one beer. At one point Wayne slipped off to the disco section of the bar. At some length he returned and announced to me: "The people here are cuckoo."

Perhaps.

A little later I went to the men's room. I was standing at the urinal when a man came up next to me, looked over, and said, "Did you really have a cat named Sloopy, and what is your philosophy of life?" Looking straight ahead, I spied the following graffito: "If America was tipped upside down, all of Southern California would land in Salt Lake City." Maybe it already had.

Passengers we are
traveling these same tracks
carried along by this same ribbon
          of boardwalk.
All journeys end
or so we are told they should.

The destination looms,
is nearly in our sights.
Can you see it, feel it?

Come closer one more time
and see it through my eyes
or stand behind me, hold on tight
and feel it through my shoulders
or feel it while I'm holding you.

I have learned in brushing up against so many people during this recent time that we are not any of us much different from each other. This is no special or illuminating truth, and I am not Columbus in my knowledge. But I do wonder if we haven't hidden so much of ourselves from each other that truth is now a by-product of fantasy and not as we suppose it should be, the other way around.

Will we ever find our father? The one who put us here and made us who we are. The one who gave us knowledge without instruction, clothes without buttons. Have I been seeking a mystery man who came together with my mother on one afternoon or evening, with me the end result, or have I all along been looking beyond that? Was there a greater need that caused a lifelong search?

Something is missing. He is missing, whoever he is. Not just in my life but in so many lives that it can't be an isolated need. If we are not on the edge of shouting out into the darkness, "Where are you, we are your children?" perhaps we should be.

Old-timers, people of other generations, some removed but one from our own, will speak about another *time of reason*. But those few who took the time to write down history do not confirm it. It isn't what's been lost but what was never learned or found, not something missing from the past that's not a part of now. It has no link with morality, science, religion, ethics, conscience, or invention. It supersedes what we know about ourselves. Maybe it isn't even what we know of right or wrong. Perhaps it has to do with a set of rules—and I don't mean manmade commandments—that were lost or not thought of before we were set down upon this place and planet. I don't even think it's mystical. In fact, I'm sure it's out there somewhere, *sound*. What is it? You tell me. Mister, if I knew I'd tell you or I'd go and find it.

There on the beach
beyond the boardwalk
two people stand
        looking into nothing.
Can't you see them?
There behind the snow-fence,
        where the track ends
            standing
            staring
some distance from each other.

One is holding little shells
and sea smooth rocks
gathered from some unnamed ocean.
The other's hands are cupped
and filled with chips of colored glass
        retrieved from that same sea.

Side by side they've come
down the same much traveled beach.
And having journeyed for a time
                on the same train
each has loped or run
the distance necessary
to have learned all lessons
        worth the learning.
Now each has gone
beyond the boardwalk separately
        not together
where something surely waits
and found that there was nothing.

Nothing is a stronger word than some might think. To begin with it is the basis for making *something*. Nothing also presupposes that there is room for a something or whatever to replace it or occupy some of its space. *Nothing* is elastic— only *no* is firm.

I am in no way unique, though I may search a different way than you, I know that you look too, even if you would deny it. Both of us, all of us, seek out the same thing. I promise you that is true. Just as I know that if one of us had found it all of us would know. It would be so level and so common that all of us would share the knowledge—whether by design or assimilation.

You cannot hide a major revelation. There has never been one except those we've made up ourselves, and when they suited us they spread like clouds to every nation. Like brushfire they could not be contained in just one country mile. All of us are looking for the Father of us all. It isn't religion, reason, genealogy. Its premise isn't even love. It is immediacy and necessity.

Long ago we learned about the mother ocean, the sea that lulls us in the cradle and the coffin. Our father is a mystery not explained away by Dad or satisfied for long by any bible.

Having found the man that I believed to be my natural father, I am quite obviously more at peace than when my search began. Questions I never thought I would ask have been brought up and answered, some before they even came to mind. I can now stop wondering and looking for that man of flesh and blood. But I will not stop looking for the other one.

I do believe that all of us are searching for the Father of us all. I intend to keep on looking. I imagine you do, too.

Birthday at Trude Heller's, 1973.

Rod and Ed Habib, 1975.

Rod and Bill Hooper, gr., 1976.

Rod with members of the immediate family, 1974.

Courtesy Hy Fujita

ABOUT THE AUTHOR

Rod McKuen's books of poetry have sold in excess of 16,0000,000 copies in hardcover, making him the bestselling and most widely read poet of our times. In addition he is the bestselling living author writing in any hardcover medium today. His poetry is taught and studied in schools, colleges, universities, and seminaries throughout the world.

Mr. McKuen is the composer of more than 1,500 songs that have been translated into Spanish, French, Dutch, German, Russian, Japanese, Czechoslovakian, Chinese, Norwegian, Afrikaans and Italian, among other languages. They account for the sale of more than 180,000,000 records. His songs include "Jean," "Love's Been Good to Me," "The Importance of the Rose," "Rock Gently," "Ally Ally, Oxen Free," and several dozen songs with French composer Jacques Brel, including "If You Go Away," "Come, Jef," "Port of Amsterdam," and "Seasons in the Sun." Both writers term their writing habits together as three distinct methods: collaboration, adaptation, and translation.

Mr. McKuen's film music has twice been nominated for Motion Picture Academy Awards *(The Prime of Miss Jean Brodie* and *A Boy Named Charlie Brown)*. His classical music, including symphonies, concertos, piano sonatas, and his very popular Adagio for Harp & Strings, is performed by leading orchestras. In May, 1972, the London Royal Philharmonic premiered his Concerto No. 3 for Piano & Orchestra, and a suite, *The Plains of My Country*. In 1973 the Louisville Orchestra commissioned Mr. McKuen to compose a suite for orchestra and narrator, entitled *The City*. It was premiered in Louisville and Danville, Kentucky, in October, 1973, and was subsequently nominated for a Pulitzer Prize in music. He has been given a new commission by the city of Portsmouth, England for a symphonic work to commemorate that city's friendship with Australia. The new work will be premiered in 1977, both in Portsmouth and in Australia's new Sydney Opera House. Mr. McKuen was the first American artist to perform a series of concerts during the opera house's opening season.

His Symphony No. 3, commissioned by the Menninger Foundation in honor of their fiftieth anniversary, was premiered in 1975 in Topeka, Kansas, and he has appeared to sell-out houses with more than thirty American symphony orchestras.

Before becoming a bestselling author and composer, Mr. McKuen worked as a laborer, radio disc jockey, and newspaper columnist, among a dozen other occupations. He spent two years in the Army, during and after the Korean War.

Rod McKuen makes his home in California in a rambling Spanish house, which he shares with a menagerie of Old English sheepdogs and a dozen cats. He likes outdoor sports and driving and has recently started taking flying lessons.

As a balloonist he has flown in the skies above the Western United States and recently South Africa. He is the subject of a new feature-length film on ballooning, entitled *Rod McKuen: Flying Free.*

The author has just completed the libretto and music for a full-length opera, *The Black Eagle.* A new book of poetry, *The Sea Around Me . . . The Hills Above,* has recently been published by Hamish Hamilton in Great Britain. *Finding My Father* is Mr. McKuen's first published book of prose. His prose work in progress is entitled *Up Hill All the Way* to be published by Coward, McCann & Geoghegan in 1977.

Much of the author's time is now spent working for and with his nonprofit foundation, Animal Concern.

The following is a list of first lines of excerpts, prose, poetry and songs appearing in *Finding My Father*, whether new or printed before.

Rod McKuen

Sources of previously published material

NEW POEMS, *Leonard* (page 65), *Mama* (page 167), *Light* (page 201), *Pictures in the Hallway* (page 203), *For My Father* (page 219), *Dinosaurs* (page 231).

From **STANYAN STREET AND OTHER SORROWS** (Published by Cheval-Stanyan Company and Random House, Inc.), *Autobiography* (pages 23, 50, and 51).

From **COME TO ME IN SILENCE** (Published by Simon and Schuster and Cheval Books, Inc.), *Entry IV* (page 26), *Sunday Two* (page 103).

From **IN SOMEONE'S SHADOW** (Published by Cheval Books, Inc., distributed by Random House, Inc.), *Alamo Junction* (page 30), *July 5* (page 115), *April 12* (page 137), *May 25* (page 173), *Prologue: Another Beginning* (page 185), *January 17* (page 195), *April 6* (page 209).

251

Rod McKuen

From **THE SEA AROUND ME . . . THE HILLS ABOVE** (Published by Hamish Hamilton, Ltd., Great Britain), *Introduction* (page 40).

From **CAUGHT IN THE QUIET** (Published by Stanyan Books and Random House, Inc.), *Seventeen* (page 41), *My Dog Likes Oranges* (page 133).

From **FIELDS OF WONDER** (Published by Cheval Books and Random House, Inc.), *I Wish I Were Seven Again* (page 53).

From **AND TO EACH SEASON** (Published by Cheval Books and Simon and Schuster), *When I Was Nine* (pages 45 and 47), *Leaving* (page 57).

From **BEYOND THE BOARDWALK** (Published by Cheval Books), *Fire Will Not Forget* (page 62), *Passengers* (pages 239 and 241).

From **THE CAROLS OF CHRISTMAS** (Published by Cheval Books and Random House, Inc.), *Conscience* (page 116).

From **LONESOME CITIES** (Published by Cheval Books and Random House, Inc.), *Cowboys/Cheyenne* (page 69), *Seattle* (page 73), *For My Son* (page 84), *The Art of Catching Trains* (page 157), *Hotel Room* (page 170).

From **ALONE** (A Bi-Plane Book, Published by Pocket Books, Inc.) and **CELEBRATIONS OF THE HEART** (Published by Cheval Books and Simon and Schuster), *Scrub Pines* (page 75).

From **LISTEN TO THE WARM,** *#34* (A Montcalm Production, Published by Random House, Inc.), (page 92).

From **MOMENT TO MOMENT** (Published by Cheval Books and Simon and Schuster), *April 5th, 9:22 A.M.* (page 97).

From **CELEBRATIONS OF THE HEART** (Published by Cheval Books and Simon and Schuster), *Report on a Life in Progress, February, 1973* (page 107).

From **SEASONS IN THE SUN** (A Bi-Plane Book, Published by Pocket Books, Inc.), *Looking Back* (page 193).

In addition, lyrics have been excerpted from the following
 songs:
LOVE CHILD (pages 31 and 34).
TO WATCH THE TRAINS (page 68).

And the aria *"The Stone Song"* from the opera **THE BLACK
 EAGLE** (page 183).